The Civil War

Through the Eyes of
Lt. Col. John Withers
and his wife
Anita Dwyer Withers

American Civil War Diaries
of a Confederate Army Officer
and His Wife, a Woman in Civil War History

Lt. Col. John Withers
Anita Dwyer Withers

with

Jennette Green

Diamond Press

THE CIVIL WAR, THROUGH THE EYES OF LT. COL. JOHN WITHERS AND HIS WIFE, ANITA DWYER WITHERS

A Diamond Press book

ISBN: 978-0-9844044-3-8

Library of Congress Control Number: 2011927272
Library of Congress Subject Headings:
Withers, John, d. 1892.
Withers, Anita Dwyer.
Withers, Anita Dwyer, fl. 1860-1865 -- Diaries.
Women -- Texas -- Diaries.
Women -- Virginia -- Diaries.
Autobiographies — Virginia.
Biography & Autobiography / Historical.
Confederate States of America. Adjutant and Inspector-General's Office.
Confederate States of America. — Army — Officers — Correspondence.
United States. — War Dept. — History — 19th century.
Confederate States of America. — Army of Northern Virginia.
United States — History — Civil War, 1861-1865 — Personal narratives, Confederate.
Richmond (Va.) — History — Civil War, 1861-1865 — Personal narratives.
Virginia — History — Civil War, 1861-1865 — Personal narratives.
Virginia — Social life and customs — 19th century.
Washington (D.C.) — Social life and customs — 19th century.
Richmond (Va.) -- Social conditions — 19th century.
Texas -- Social life and customs -- 19th century.
Theater — United States — History — 19th century.
Catholic Church — Virginia — History — 19th century.
Generals — Confederate States of America.

Diamond Press
3400 Pegasus Drive
P.O. Box 80043
Bakersfield CA 93380-0043
www.diamondpresspublishing.com

Published in the United States of America.

Contents

Acknowledgements

Many people have made this book possible, and I would like to thank as many as I can here. First of all, I would like to thank the National Archives, which has carefully preserved so many of our nation's historical records. Each one is an important piece of our national heritage.

A few months ago, I discovered the images of Lt. Col. John Withers' diary on the National Archives website. I was amazed that his story had not been published before. As I went beyond his diary and researched more of his life, I soon learned that Withers was an extremely well-liked and respected man. He was also closely acquainted with many of the notable people of Civil War history, and his diary is rich in facts and detail of that time period. It is a fascinating read.

While researching the background for Lt. Col. Withers' book, I discovered that his wife, Anita Dwyer Withers, already had her Civil War diary transcribed by the University of North Carolina at Chapel Hill. It is available online. It has been a rewarding and fascinating journey to weave together Lt. Col. Withers and Anita's diaries to create a multi-dimensional picture of the Withers' lives together during the Civil War.

Thank you to everyone at UNC-CH for making Anita's diary available to all. Special thanks to Jim Crawford, who scanned the text via OCR, and to J.G. McKim and Natalia Smith, who encoded the text.

Last, but certainly not least, I would like to give heartfelt thanks to Glenna Jo Christen of Mrs. Christen's Miscellanea in southeast Michigan, for taking the photo of the lovely Marie Stewart bonnet on the cover of this book. Much appreciation and thanks also to the talented Salli Thompson, who made the gorgeous bonnet. Without both of you, this cover for the book would not have been possible!

Introduction

This book weaves together the diaries of Lt. Col. John Withers, an Assistant Adjutant General for Jefferson Davis, and his wife, Anita Dwyer Withers. Reports of battles fought meld with domestic life in these journals, creating a multi-dimensional picture of the Withers' lives together during the "War Between the States." Jointly, their diaries encompass the entire length of the Civil War; from May 1860 – September 1865.

A West Point graduate, John Withers served as an officer in the U.S. Army in Michigan, New York, California, Washington, Oregon, and Texas. As a Brevet Captain in 1857, Withers was appointed as Staff-Assistant Adjutant General for the Department of Texas.

Captain John Withers' wife, Anita Dwyer Withers, was "the daughter of a very distinguished citizen of San Antonio, and who was connected with the exciting scenes that delivered Texas from Mexican rule and Indian terror," later wrote John Withers' friend, D.S. Stanley. Anita married John on June 15, 1859.

In September 1860, six months after the birth of their first child, Captain Withers was ordered to Washington, D.C., and assigned for duty as an Assistant in the Adjutant-General's office. As Anita was very close to her family in Texas, she was deeply troubled by the move. She wrote, "I regret it mightily." In Washington, D.C., John served under General Samuel Cooper's command until March, 1861.

John Withers' family was from the south. His uncle, Clement Comer Clay, was the 8th Governor of Alabama, (and also in his lifetime, Chief Justice of Alabama, Congressman, and U. S. Senator). When Withers received a letter from his aunt, Susanna Withers Clay (Clement Clay's wife), urging him to resign his commission in the U.S. Army and come south to join the Confederate cause, Withers did so. He joined the Confederate Army in March, 1861, and "was appointed a Major in the Adjutant-General's Department." (Stanley)

As an Assistant Adjutant General working in Richmond, VA, both Lt. Col. Withers and his wife were closely acquainted with many of the notable figures of Civil War history, including C.S.A. President Jefferson Davis, his wife, Varina Davis, and the Secretary of War. Edward A. Palfrey later wrote, "his relations with the President and Secretary of War were of an intimate character, as was necessarily the case from the position he held." In addition, Withers mentioned meetings with famous Confederate Generals Robert E. Lee, Joe E. Johnston, A.S. Johnston, and others. He casually alluded to other heads of state that he met as a matter of course in his position.

While stationed in the Confederate capitol of Richmond, Virginia, both Anita and Lt. Col. Withers recorded Civil War events as they happened, including the Seven Days Battles, and other battles that took place during the "War Between the States." Each also wrote of the more personal aspects of their lives, such as Anita's near fatal illness and the agony of their young son's death.

Anita's diary records the family's transition from Texas to Washington D.C., then to Richmond, VA, and later to Texas again near the end of the war. In all, her journal records events from May 1860 – September 1865. Many selected excerpts from her diary are included, which complements Lt. Col. John Withers' journal (October 1860 – December 1862).

Both Lt. Col. John Withers and Anita's diaries provide a detailed Civil War timeline rich in facts and details. John and Anita were ordinary people living in extraordinary times. Their story is well worth being remembered.

May – July, 1860.

Anita's Diary.

<u>May 4th. 1860</u>. May the 1st. was the first time that I went down to breakfast with my Husband since the birth of our baby. That morning I practised on the Piano, and took a ride in the afternoon.

<u>May 4th.</u> All well (T G) Mrs. Mitchell, Miss Conrad, Miss Post, and Miss Rodriguez called to see me, they were all delighted with little Edward. We took a short drive. My Mother came over in the evening to take care of the baby so that I might go and hear the Swiss bell Ringers but I did not care to attend.

<u>May 7th.</u> A very windy day. The Capt. and myself made a few visits today, for the first time since the birth of my Edward.

<u>May 10th. Thursday.</u> A beautiful day, our bath house was completed today, it is a mighty nice one. My Mother and myself went down to see it this morning. Ma bought the baby a sweet little hat at $4. We had a number of calls today, and we took a drive in the evening. The Captain was planting Water melons all the afternoon.

<u>May 14th. Monday.</u> Quite warm and close today. I stayed at home as usual all the morning. In the afternoon we took the baby out driv-

ing for the first time, he paid Miss Conrad a visit, they were all delighted to see him, he behaved exceedingly well, didn't cry at all. Capt. and Mrs. Lee called whilst we were out. We remained at home in the evening.

<u>May 22nd. Tuesday.</u> Today the baby is two months old, his Papa weighed him and he has gained 2 lbs this last month. He now weighs 11 lbs.

<u>June 15th.</u> The Anniversary of our marriage, we have been married a year 1860. In the morning we arranged the house for an entertainment. Miss Aurelia and Mrs. Mickling came in today to assist me. They made the chicken salad and got Joe [Anita's brother] to help them. We set the table very prettily in the afternoon. I have had the headache all day, and got worse in the evening. I was obliged to leave the company and go upstairs to bed. About half past seven we went to the New Church with the baby, a great number of persons were already there. The Church was all lighted very prettily. Father Shean performed the ceremony. The party went off very well, although the Captain sent the Mexican musicians off. Joe played Robert on the Violin and I accompanied him on the Piano.

<u>June 19th. Tuesday.</u> The Capt., baby and myself took a ride before breakfast. In the afternoon I made a few calls, went to the casita and took a drive with Joe and the Captain. After Tea Joe and Capt. went to call on Col. Lee—and Mr. Toutant. Joe talked about Miss Whitely and made my Mother mad.

<u>June 20th. Wednesday.</u> The Capt., baby and myself took a drive before breakfast. My Ma and myself went to see Isabelle Casiano who

has a young baby. Joe was fined 6 dollars today for galloping on horseback in town.

<u>July 22nd.</u> Joe, my Ma and myself went to six o'clock Mass, I lost a little veil I had. Today the baby Edward is four months old, he weighs 13 and a half pounds. My Mother, the Capt, Joe, Myself, Charlotte with the baby went out to Major Dashiell's after our siesta. We had a nice moonlight drive returning. After Tea my Ma, Capt. and Joe commenced talking about the cattle on the Ranch, upon which topic my Mother got mad and went home.

September, 1860.

<u>Sept. 6th.</u> *The Captain received an order to go to Washington quite unexpectedly to us. I regret it mightily.*

<u>Sept. 14th. Friday.</u> *We left home for Washington by the way of Columbus. My brother came a part of the way with us. I hated to leave my Mother and home greatly.*

<u>Sept. 27th.</u> *We arrived in Huntsville. They were all glad to see us.... The baby is sick, we sent for a Doctor on the 29th. On the 28th. I was obliged to wean Edward much to my sorrow.*

October, 1860.

Lt. Col. John Withers' Journal.

<u>Monday, 1st.</u> Anita, Edward and I, left Huntsville about 7, A.M., on our way to Washington: we traveled all day and night. Edward was pretty well during the day, but was not so at night.

<u>Tuesday, 2nd.</u> We again traveled all day and night, although our little boy had fever nearly the whole time.

<u>Wednesday, 3rd.</u> We reached Washington City about daylight, and put up at Brown's Hotel. I reported at the Adjutant General's Office after breakfast, and then went house hunting. The Prince of Wales, and Suite, arrived here at 5, P.M., and went to the President's.

<u>Anita: October 3rd. Wednesday.</u> *We arrived in Washington, and stopped at Brown's where we spent nearly a fortnight. My baby is sick all the time, Dr. Edwards is attending him.*

<u>Thursday, 4th.</u> In company with the other officers of the Army, as well as the Navy Officers, all in full dress Uniform, I went up to the President's at 12, M., to-day, and paid my respects to

Lord Renfrew: I bowed to him, and he to me, as I passed him. I shook hands with Mr. Buchanan and Secretary Floyd. The reception room was jammed with people. The Prince is a pleasant looking, amiable appearing young man, with a big nose. I had seen the Prince and suite pass down Pennsylvania Avenue earlier in the day, on his way to visit the capitol and other public buildings.

Friday, 5th. Baron Renfrew, the Prince of Wales, went to Mount Vernon with his suite to-day. Nothing special going on except the magnificent display of fire works near the President's in the evening: Anita and I saw a portion of them.

Saturday, 6th. The Prince of Wales and suite left to-day for Richmond, Virginia. Anita and I both saw them as they passed down Pennsylvania Avenue.

Sunday, 7th. Anita and I attended St. Aloysius church to-day, and heard a splendid sermon by Father McGuire.

Sunday, 14th. During the past week I have been busy house hunting, and finally determined to take a furnished one, No. 261, "I" St., between 17th and 18th. We have been much worried all the week on account of Edward's being indisposed— he is much better to-day. It is raining and quite cool, cold I might say, and we have fire in our room.

Monday, 15th. We moved from the Hotel to our rented house on I Street, between 17th and 18th to-day: we had no wood, coal or gas, but succeeded in getting the former two before night. We are very nicely fixed on the whole. I was down in the city a while in the earlier part of the afternoon, but remained at home at night. Pleasant weather.

Tuesday, 16th. Anita and I were engaged getting our groceries, and other little necessaries for house keeping. We have gas to-night. Our cook and chamber-maid answer our purposes very well. Pleasant day. Frost.

Wednesday, 17th. Our little son is better to-day—we took him out in the carriage with us as we went visiting: we made half a dozen calls. Fine weather. We are faily [sic] house keeping again. Mrs. Genl. Is. Johnston called to see Anita sociably late in the afternoon.

Thursday, 18th. Anita and I took Edward out visiting with us to-day, although he was quite sick last night—the ride in the open air seemed to do him good, but he got worse again late in the afternoon. The doctor came whilst the little fellow was suffering, and seemed to understand at once what was troubling him: he made a prescription for him which relieved his pain and put him to sleep. Mr. Calvert, the gentleman from whom I rented our house, spent the evening with us.

Friday, 19th. Cloudy and windy all day: rained hard at night. I wrote letters all the evening. Our little boy is very much better indeed. Nothing going on. Mrs. Dr. Wood called to see Anita to-day. The storm was very severe at night.

Saturday, 20th. Rainy, disagreeable day. I was at home most of the day and at night. Edward is very much better.

Sunday, 21st. Anita and I went to St. Matthews Church in the forenoon, and took the baby out riding after dinner. Fine day. We consider Edward well now. Dr. Wood called to-day.

Anita: October 21st. Sunday. *The Captain and myself went to St. Mathiews Church this morning at 11 O'clock. The baby is a great deal better, I might say well since yesterday. Thank God. We dined early today so as to give the servants time to go out. After dinner the Captain hired a carriage and took Eddie, nurse and myself to Georgetown. We saw some sweet places on the heights. After Tea we took a walk, the Captain wrote to Joe.*

Monday, 22nd. Pleasant day. I was duly installed at my desk in the Adjutant General's Office to-day. Anita and I walked out in the afternoon, and I walked down the avenue after tea. Our baby is seven months old to-day: he was not well last night, and kept us up until about three O'Clock.

Tuesday, 23rd. I was at the Office until 3, P.M. Anita and I walked down the avenue after dinner, and I called to see Genl. Harney after tea. I found the General alone—he has rooms at a negro man's named Wormley. We sat and talked for about two hours.

Wednesday, 24th. Anita walked down in the City before dinner, with Charlotte and the baby: I found her complaining of fatigue when I came from the Office, she ate only a little dinner, and then went to bed. I remained at home all the afternoon. Lt. and Mrs. A.P. Hill, and Capt. Williams called at night and sat an hour or so. After they left I went down for Dr. Edwards, who came up to see Anita—he gave her a dover powder to take, which nauseated her and made her vomit.

Thursday, 25th. Anita had violent headache and nausea this morning, and spit up a little blood in her efforts to vomit. I remained at home with her all day: she got some better by noon, and was much improved by night, but still kept her bed.

Friday, 26th. Anita was better in the morning, and continued to improve all day. I was at the office to-day, and called in the evening to see Mr. Bell, and to bid Maj. and Mrs. Nichols goodbye.

Saturday, 27th. Neither Col. Cooper, Maj. Townsend nor Capt. Williams were at the office to-day, so Capt. Garesché and I had it all to our own way. I took Anita and Edward out riding in the afternoon. Beautiful days and moonlight nights—the nights are not bright as we have them in Texas, there being much more moisture in the air here than there. Nothing very interesting going on.

Sunday, 28th. Anita and I walked to church at ten O'Clock, but we could not get a seat and returned home: in the afternoon we went down to the laying of the corner stone of the St. Aloisius Orphan's Asylum, and heard a sermon by the Rev. Father McGuire. There were several thousand persons present. McLean and Ihrie came around in the evening: Dr. Smith, Dr. Foard, and A.P. Hill were around to see us during the day. Cloudy nearly all day, and strong indication of rain, but no rain fell.

Monday, 29th. I was at the Office from nine, A.M., until three, P.M. Anita, and Charlotte with Edward, walked down the avenue, and did not get back home until near four O'Clock. I called at Col. Craig's and to see Capt. Williams, Dr. Foard and Capt. Alexander after dinner: we remained at home all the evening.

Anita: Oct. 29th. Monday. I took the baby and Charlotte with me down town, took the omnibus first and went to see the Capitol, and afterwards I went shopping, and was obliged to walk back home, much to my dislike.

Tuesday, 30th. Rained last night, and a little this afternoon. Anita and I called at Dr. Wood's and at Dr. Smith's in the afternoon. I called to see Capt. and Mrs. McLean in the evening.

Wednesday, 31st. Rained hard last night and a little to-day. I walked around to see Mr. and Mrs. A.P. Hill after tea. Bell and Trowbridge called, the former in the afternoon, the latter at night. My pay, Col. T.P. Andrews, was $157.60, and my commutation, Capt. Morris Miller, was $43.00. Anita's rents were $85. My transportation (Capt. Morris Miller), from San Antonio, Texas, to Washington City, D.C., for self and servant, was $252.05. Our income was, therefore, $537.65. Our expenses amounted to $517.24. Our income exceeded our expenses by $20.41.

November, 1860.

Thursday, 1st. I was at the Office until three, P.M. After dinner Anita and I called to see Mrs. Jacob Thompson, Mrs. Phillips and Mrs. McLean, and in the evening we called at Capt. Garesché's. I afterward called to see Dr. Cuyler, at Judge Wayne's and Genl. Harney at his quarters. Beautiful, moonlight night.

Friday, 2nd. Capt. and Mrs. Samuel Jones called about 3 P.M. I went down town after dinner to pay for my houserent, gas, ale, &c. Damp and drizzly pretty much all day.

Saturday, 3rd. Rainy again to-day: no one can get out for exercise [in] such weather. At night it got cool and stopped raining, and Anita and I took a short walk. Anita put short dresses on Edward to-day for the first time—he looks even more cunning than ever. I wrote several private letters to-day.

Sunday, 4th. Anita and I went to St. Aloisius Church in the morning, and heard a beautifully eloquent sermon from the Rev. Father Clark. In the evening we called to see Mrs. Hill but she was unwell and we did not meet her. Beautiful day.

Anita: November 4th. Went to Mass to St. Aloysius with the Capt. The Rev'd Mr. Clarke preached a beautiful sermon on Heaven.

Monday, 5th. Nothing of interest going on, except a probable chance of an order to send Genl. Johnston to California instead of to Texas. I called to see Genl. Johnston at Kirkwood's in the evening. Wrote to Aunt Clay and Mr. Battle to-day.

Tuesday, 6th. The Election for President and Vice President is going on in the different States to-day: everything is quiet here on the surface, though I have no doubt there is really more excitement than in any other city of its size in the Union. I walked down in the city at night, but heard no news of any consequence. Quite cold to-day. Mrs. Jacob Thompson, wife of the Secretary, called to see Anita to-day.

Anita: November 6th. Mr. Lincoln I regret to say is elected President of the United States. What will become of us.

Wednesday, 7th. Enough returns have been received to satisfy everyone that Lincoln is elected President. Beautiful day — cool. Mrs. and Miss Ingraham, General A.S. Johnston, Lieut. Bell, Maj. Belger and Mr. Duff called to see Anita to-day — the latter two spent an hour or so in the evening. I walked down in the City with Bell a little after dark.

Thursday, 8th. Anita and I walked down the avenue to make some purchases in the afternoon: the day was bracing, so she wore her shawl, and I my overcoat. At night I went to the Theater and heard Jefferson as Bob Acres in "The Rivals." Genl. Johnston, (A.S.), and I sat together. After the close of the play the Genl. asked me to a restaurant to take some oysters — after enjoying these, and sitting with the Genl. at his Hotel for half an hour or so, I came home. This is the first time I have been to a Theatrical performance, I believe, for at least a year.

Friday, 9th. Rained nearly all day—mild. Ingalls called at the Office this morning, looking as natural as ever. I was quite busy at the Office to-day; more so, perhaps, than any day since I have had charge.

Saturday, 10th. Rained to-day again: at night I called at Kirkwood's to see Ingalls and Rankin, but they were out. Anita was not well to-day, or to-night. Edward is getting quite fat.

Sunday, 11th. Cool and cloudy. We went to church in the morning, and called to see Mrs. McLean in the evening. Wife and baby well.

Anita: November [10 -] 12th. *The Captain and myself went to Church at 11 O'clock round to St. Mathews we had no sermon. In the afternoon we played with Edward and then took a nap, at night I wrote to Joe and gave him a good scolding for not writing oftener. (I put Edward in short clothes on the 10th. of November, Saturday.)*

Monday, 12th. At the Office as usual—took a nap after dinner. Capt. and Mrs. Garesché, and Mrs. Garesché's sister, called to see Anita just before night.

Tuesday, 13th. I left the Office at noon to-day, and took Anita and the baby over to Arlington—the ladies (Lee's) were out, and we had to return without seeing anyone. Dr. and Mrs. Chs. Smith, Miss Smith and her niece, and Mr. and Mrs. A.P. Hill, called in the evening to see Anita. We had just returned from a visit to Dr. Wood's when some of our visitors came. Anita and I called at several places in the afternoon, at Mr. Floyd's amongst the rest: we saw Mrs. Floyd, and her little granddaughter. Beautiful day—clear and cool, without being cold.

Anita: Tuesday 13th. A beautiful day. The Capt. and myself, baby and Char. went out Arlington to see Mrs. Col. Lee, but we found everybody away; on our return we went to see Mrs. Bell and the McCormick's, also Mrs. Secretary Floyd, Mrs. Trobridge, Mrs. S. Jones, and Mrs. Craig. After Tea we called at Mrs. Wood's and on our return home found Dr. and Mrs. Smith and the Miss Smiths at home, Mr. and Mrs. A. P. Hill also came round.

Wednesday, 14th. I was at the Office until 3, P.M. Walked down the avenue after dinner. Lovely day. Anita and I went to a concert at Willard's Hall in the evening, and heard Madame Fabbri, Signor Stigelli (Tenor) and Carl Formes (Bass), with Mulder as pianist. The audience was select, and the music very fine indeed. Formes' voice is the finest bass I ever heard.

Anita: Wednesday. November 14th. The Captain and myself went to the Concert to hear Fabbri, Stigelli, and Carl Formes, the latter had the finest bass voice I ever heard.

Thursday, 15th. Called at Capt. Palmer's and at Capt. Miller's after dinner. We went to the theatre at night, and heard Jefferson in "Our American Cousin": he is a fine comedian.

Anita: Thursday 15th. We went to hear Jefferson in the American Cousin, I was greatly pleased, but what amused me most was the

English Lord of Londreary acting the silly "Thats the idea." We drove home in a carriage.

<u>*Friday, 16th.*</u> We walked down the avenue in the morning, and I went down to see Mr. Duff off for Texas in the afternoon. Capt. and Mrs. McLean spent the evening with us. Cloudy and cool all day, but no rain.

<u>*Saturday, 17th.*</u> Rained all day. I walked down to Dr. Edwards' after tea, and sat with him an hour or so.

<u>*Sunday, 18th.*</u> Anita and I went to church in the morning, and I went down to see Mr. Duff off for Texas in the afternoon. Capt. and Mrs. McLean spent the evening with us. Cloudy and cool all day, but no rain.

<u>*Anita: Nov. 18th. Sunday.*</u> *We went to St. Mathiews at 11 O'clock. After dinner I took a nap, the Captain went to see Mr. Duff off, and Charlotte took the baby out for a little while. Edward can sit up alone now.*

<u>*Monday, 19th.*</u> I was at the Office as usual. Anita and I called to see Mrs. Clary, Mrs. Ray, and Mrs. Sibley, in the afternoon, and Mrs. Phillips in the evening. Cloudy, but pleasant, rather. Nothing special going on.

<u>*Tuesday, 20th.*</u> At the Office as usual. I walked down the Avenue in the afternoon, and Anita and I went to hear Christy's Minstrels in the evening: great crowd, a squeeze in fact, and the music very good.

Anita: Tuesday, 20th. We went to hear G. Christy the Negro Minstrels, they had a crowded house. I found very amusing, they had some very good Music.

Wednesday, 21st. I walked down the avenue after dinner, and Anita and I went to Mr. McCormick's to see Mrs. McCormick and her daughter Nannie, who have just arrived from California. Mrs. McCormick is not well, and Nannie is not so pretty as she was when a girl. Right cool.

Anita: Wednesday, 21st. The Captain and myself went round to Mrs. Gwinn after Tea, they were exceedingly kind and polite. We met Secretary Cobb and his lady there. After our visit there, we went to Mr. McCormick's to see Mrs. Dr. McCormick and Nannie, who have just gotten back from California.

Thursday, 22nd. I went with Mrs. McCormick and Nannie in the morning to hunt a boarding house—they took rooms at Mrs. Bryant's. Anita and I called at Commander Ingraham's and at Gov. Stevens' in the afternoon. Quite cold to-day, and at night.

Friday, 23rd. Rained all day. Anita and I took a nap after dinner—she is not very well to-day.

Saturday, 24th. Very cold to-day, and at night. Genl. Joe Johnston came around and spent an hour or so with us after tea. Beautiful moonlight night.

Sunday, 25th. Anita and I went to church in the forenoon, and I went around to see Mrs. McCormick and Nannie at Mrs. Bryants' after tea. Clear and cold.

Monday, 26th. At the Office as usual. Anita and I walked down in the city after dinner, and called at Dr. Smith's after tea. Cloudy and cool, but not cold like yesterday and the day before.

Tuesday, 27th. Cloudy and mild. I called to see Maj. Belger after tea: he lately had a tumor taken from his right shoulder.

Wednesday, 28th. Busy at the Office as usual. I walked down the avenue after dinner. Cleared off beautifully in the afternoon: beautiful, moonlight night.

Thursday, 29th. This is Thanksgiving day. I went to the Office, opened the mail, and came back home. Anita went to St. Matthews' (Catholic) and I went to the church of the Epiphany, (Episcopalian). We dined at Lt. A.P. Hill's, with Capt. Wm. F. Smith. After dinner we had a game of whist with some gentlemen who were invited round. Hill took Anita home about ten O'Clock, and I remained to play until midnight. Altogether we spent a most agreeable day and evening. As usual, when we are out, persons called to see us. Mrs. Jefferson Davis and Capt. Williams called, both of whom we would like to have met.

Friday, 30th. Our dear little Edward has not been well to-day. Towards evening he seemed to be better. Rained at intervals during the day and evening. I walked down in the City after dinner, paying my monthly dues (or what I was duing [sic]). Mr. Calvert (our Landlord) called in the evening to collect *his* dues, which were also paid by the undersigned: he took several cups of tea with us. Capt. Seth Williams, Asst. Adjt. Genl., called to bid us farewells in the evening, although he had called yesterday: he and I joined in a parting glass.

My pay, Col. Andrews, was $155.50: My commutation, Capt. Miller, was $46.00, and Anita's rents were $85.00. Our income was, therefore, $286.50. Our expenses were $319.43. Our expenses exceeded our income by $32.93.

December, 1860.

<u>Saturday, 1st.</u> At the Office as usual. Took Anita to church after dinner, and then walked down the avenue to attend to some errands: called to see Mrs. McCormick and Nannie on my return home. Went to call on Senator and Mrs. Davis after tea: Met several persons there.

<u>Sunday, 2nd.</u> Anita went to communion this morning, and I went to the church of the Epiphany (Episcopal). Cold and windy. After dinner Anita and I went upstairs to take a nap: we had just gotten to bed (about 4, P.M.) when some one rang the door bell, and, when the door was opened, in came Sister Mary. She came on from Huntsville with the Hon. Geo. S. Houston, Member Congress from Alabama, who also had under his charge a young lady (Miss Boggs) from Philadelphia. Anita, Mary and I were all delighted at our meeting of course. Mary says the cars were thrown from the track yesterday morning, by a snake head, and a negro man who jumped off was killed: those who remained inside were only frightened. It was a merciful escape for all the rest. After tea I went down to Brown's to call on Geo. Houston. I met him, Miss Boggs, Mrs. Fitzpatrick, Mrs. Cobb, and others.

Monday, 3rd. At the Office as usual. Both houses of Congress assembled, organized and adjourned, to await the reception of the President's message. Mary and Anita made some visits during the day. I called to see Mrs. Gov. Fitzpatrick, and Capt. and Mrs. McLean about night. Pleasant day and night.

Tuesday, 4th. The ground was covered about two inches with snow this morning when we got up. Cleared off during the day: not very cold. Wm. E. Jones, a classmate of mine, who resigned some years since, came to see me at the Office to-day, and afterward dined with us: he and I called at Dr. Smith's after dinner. The President submitted his message to-day—he takes the ground that no State has a right to secede, but that the Federal Government has no right to coerce one of its members back after withdrawal.

Wednesday, 5th. The snow did not melt a great deal to-day, not-withstanding it was a bright day, and not atall cold: fine night. I took a nap after dinner, and called with Jones to see Mrs. McCormick after tea. Anita and Mary walked down in the city during the day—they took a carriage before going far, having found the walking bad.

Tuesday, 6th. Walked on the Avenue with Anita and Mary before dinner—commenced to dine at 5, instead of 3 P.M. We called to see Mrs. Wigfall in the evening. Pleasant day, and evening. Anita discovered to-day that our little boy has a tooth through.

Friday, 7th. A volunteer company, the Putnam Phalanx, were reviewed by President Buchanan to-day, in front of the

Presidential Mansion, and afterwards were entertained by the President. Anita, Mary and I went over to Georgetown in the afternoon, and visited the Jesuit College: we saw the President, Father Early, and young Abadie and Donegan—the latter from Huntsville. Fine day. I walked down to Willard's after tea and called on some Officers: I afterwards called by to see Mrs. McCormick, to invite she and Nannie to-dine with us to-morrow.

Saturday, 8th. Rainy and disagreeable all day. Mrs. McCormick and Nannie were unable to come to dine on account of the weather, and Anita was too unwell with sick headache to come to the table. Lieut. Graham, and Mr. Abadie dined with us. Lt. Hartsuff called after dinner. We had a very excellent dinner indeed, and enjoyed it exceedingly. I remained at home all the evening. Nothing special going on in the Office.

Sunday, 9th. I went to St. Aloisius Church, and heard a fine sermon from Father Clark on the Immaculate Conception. Anita and Mary remained at home—Anita was not very well in the morning, but was much better in the afternoon and at night. I remained at home all the evening. Not cold, but cloudy.

Monday, 10th. Raining and disagreeable all day. I called to see Mrs. McCormick and Capt. Ingalls after tea.

Tuesday, 11th. Anita, Mary and I called, after tea, to see Mrs. Hill, Mrs. Henry and Mrs. Mayuadier, but met none of them. Pleasant day, and clear at night: it is cold and damp every night, however.

Wednesday, 12th. Anita's Piano, and our books reached us to-day. In the evening Anita, Mary and I went to hear a musical prodigy in a negro boy Tom, apparently about eleven or twelve years of age, who is blind, has never received any instruction, and yet who plays the piano exquisitely—executing the most difficult operatic pieces, and playing anything that he hears played once. He played two pieces at once, Fishers Hornpipe with his right hand and Yankee Doodle with his left, in perfect time, and carried on a conversation at the same time. He also played with his back to the piano. Altogether, he is a most extraordinary boy.

Thursday, 13th. We had the piano box opened this morning, and the piano brought into the parlor: it was in good order exteriorly, and in very good tune—quite as good I think, as when we left San Antonio. We had several visitors in the evening.

Friday, 14th. We opened the boxes containing our books to-day, and found the books in good order. Clear and cold, day and night. I called to see Mrs. McCormick after tea. General Scott has been in the City several days, and recommends that reinforcements be sent to Charleston harbor. General Cass has entertained like views, and resigned his place in the Cabinet to-day, in consequence of the failure of the President to adopt this policy.

Saturday, 15th. Snowing fast when we waked this morning, and continued to do so most of the day. I saw General Scott, and shook hands with him, as he was going from his Office about two, P.M., to see the President. Remained at home all the evening. A stable fired and burned up just across the street from our house about eight O'Clock at night: a great crowd of men, women and children were congregated, as always happens on such occasions.

Sunday, 16th. Anita, Mary and I went to St. Aloisius in the morning. Beautiful day. Took a nap after dinner, and walked down to Brown's after tea.

Monday, 17th. Snow melting fast—not cold. In the afternoon I walked down to Brown's, and saw Genl. Houston of Alabama, and Genl. Moore also. The Secession convention of South Carolina meets to-day. Senator Wade of Ohio made a speech in Senate to-day, on the abolition side of our present troubles—it was very mild in tone for him, I understand.

Tuesday, 18th. Busy at the Office all day. Capts. Floyd-Jones, and Burton, and Lt. Piper called at the Office to-day. I took a walk down the avenue after dinner. W.E. Jones called a little after dark, and took a cup of tea with us. Captain Jordan and Lt. Saxton called after tea, and remained until midnight. Mary and Anita left us about ten P.M., and went to bed.

Wednesday, 19th. I was not atall well to-day, and did not go to the Office: Jordon Saxton and I must have taken too many toddies last night. Drizzling rain pretty much all day, which will no doubt melt off nearly all the remaining snow.

Thursday, 20th. I was at my Office as usual. Nothing of special importance going on.

Friday, 21st. I was at my Office as usual. Just after returning home at three, P.M., I received a message from Colonel Cooper asking me to return to the Office. He gave me a package which he said the President wished me to deliver to Major Robert Anderson, 1st Arty., commanding Fort Moultrie, S. Carolina. I came home, got my carpet sack ready, and left for Charleston at seven P.M.: traveled all night.

Saturday, 22nd. Traveled all day and all night.

Sunday, 23rd. Arrived in Charleston about half after nine O'Clock, A.M., took breakfast, and went to the wharf to go over to Sullivan's Island. The Steamer had left, but I went over in a boat (private) with General Jamison, President of the South Carolina Convention, and Messrs: Cheves, Gregg and Dr. Green, members of the same. I introduced them to Major Anderson, and they were very polite to him and he to them. Genl. Jamison gave Maj. Anderson a written permit to attend the Convention. I took dinner with Major Anderson, saw the Officers in the Fort, took a look around the Fort, and went over to Charleston late in the afternoon. Met a Mr. Butter whom I had known in the Cherokee Country many years since — he is a member of the State Legislature, and a son in law of Gov. Pickens. He introduced me to the Gov. and Mrs. Pickens, and the Lieut. Governor, Col. Harney. I left Charleston at eleven, P.M., and traveled all night. Beautiful weather.

Monday, 24th. Traveled all day and all night.

Tuesday, 25th. Reached Washington at two, P.M., reported my return to Secretary Floyd, and got home at three O'Clock, P.M.

Had a merry Christmas dinner with My dear wife and Sister Mary, and reported to the President after tea.

Wednesday, 26th. At my Office as usual. In the evening Anita, Mary and I went to an Operatic concert by Madame Colson, Signors Brignoli, Ferri and Susini, with Musio as Conductor. We expected much, and received little: to us it was an unmitigated failure.

Thursday, 27th. I was at my Office as usual, with the exception of an hour in the forenoon which I took to accompany Anita and Mary to the Senate. They heard Mr. Doolittle make a speech. It is a delightful day. News was received to-day that Major Anderson evacuated Fort Moultrie last night, and occupies Fort Sumter with his command — he is reported to have spiked the guns, and burned their carriages before leaving the former Fort. The Officers of the Army whom I have seen, except Major John F. Lee, Judge Advocate, laud Maj. Anderson for this act. The Southern Members of Congress deprecate the act, as a matter of course.

Friday, 28th. It is reported to-day that the South Carolinians have taken possession of Fort Moultrie and Castle Pinckney. In the evening I called to see Mr. and Mrs. Yulee, Mr. and Mrs. Gwin, and Mr. and Mrs. Davis; Captain D.R. Jones and Genl. Gibson I called to see in the afternoon. I have a bad cold and sore throat.

Saturday, 29th. Nothing unusual going on to-day. Mr. Floyd resigned his position as Secretary of War to-day, in consequence, it is surmised, of the refusal of the President to withdraw Major Anderson from Fort Sumter.

<u>*Sunday, 30th.*</u> Rained all day, and at night. I remained at home all day—as did Anita and Mary.

<u>*Monday, 31st.*</u> I was at the Office as usual, though I had a most severe cold: I went to bed when I returned home at three O'Clock, and did not get up until night. Charlotte, our nurse, has been quite ill all day, with something like pneumonia. Sally, our house girl, had a violent tooth-ache, which incapacitated her for any duty until after dinner—she had the tooth extracted. Our dear Edward, too, has been unwell all day: Charlotte says he is cutting another tooth. I remained at home at night. We had a pretty heavy fall of snow last night, and everything is clothed in white to-day.

My pay, Col. T. P. Andrews, was $157.60. My commutation, Capt. Miller, was $46.00. My transportation to Charleston, and back, was $119.00. Anita's rents amounted to $105. Our income amounted, therefore, to $427.60. Our expenses amounted to $472.02. Our expense exceeded our income by $44.42.

January, 1861.

<u>*Tuesday, 1st.*</u> The Officers of the Army and Navy, the former headed by General Scott, and all in full Uniform, were presented to the President at a quarter before noon to-day; the Members of the Cabinet, and Diplomatic corps, with their wives were present. The general reception took place from noon until 2, P.M. I made several calls after going to the President's, and went to see Mrs. Colonel Bonneville amongst the rest. It was a bright day over head, but the streets were wet and slippery. It has been, altogether, not an agreeable New Years day to me and my family. Our little boy has a bad cold. I have the same, and our old nurse Charlotte is in bed with the same. We officers of the Army could not call upon Genl. Scott—he was so much exhausted by the effort of going to the President's that he returned to his quarters to go to bed. Mr. Holt, the Post Master General, is to be acting Secretary of War, in place of Mr. Floyd resigned. We all remained at home in the evening, and retired early on account of the indisposition of several members of the household. Cold at night.

<u>*Wednesday, 2nd.*</u> I was at the Office as usual to-day, took a walk with Anita down the avenue after dinner, and remained at home in the evening. Foggy in the morning, mild and cloudy in the afternoon, and raining at night. There was a

very large fire on the avenue last night, by which six large stores were destroyed.

Thursday, 3rd. Busy at the Office as usual. Saw General Scott in Col. Cooper's room. Nothing of special importance going on. Called to see Hazen, and some other Officers at Willard's after tea. Charlotte and Edward are still suffering from colds.

Friday, 4th. I merely opened the mail, and left the Office for the day—this being a day set apart by President Buchanan as one for fasting, humiliation and prayer. Remained at home all day.

Saturday, 5th. I left the Office about half after one O'Clock, P.M. Anita and I went up to a reception at Col. Craig's about half after two, P.M: the Colonel's daughter was married recently to Maj. Hunt, of the 1st Artillery, and it was their reception, or rather hers, as the Major has been ordered off upon some secret service, and was not at the reception. We met many of our friends in and out of the Army. Beautiful day. I walked down the Avenue after dinner—met Mrs. McCormick, Nannie and her little cousin Annie Nells from Annapolis.

Sunday, 6th. Anita and I went to church at St. Aloisius: she was quite unwell all day, with sick headache. I walked down to the hotel (Brown's) after tea, to see if I could hire a cook, and found that Cousin Clement and Cousin Jeannie had arrived here yesterday afternoon. I went up to their room, and remained until about ten O'Clock. Cousin Clement looks very much better than I had expected to have seen him, and Cousin Jeannie looks remarkably well.

Monday, 7th. In the afternoon Anita, Mary and I went to the hotel to see Cousin Jeannie. We left about half after seven to go to the theater, where we saw Hackett as Falstaff in Henry IV. It was an admirable performance: a crowded audience.

Tuesday, 8th. Mary and I went to hear Hackett as Sir Pertinax Mac Sycophant, in the Man of the World. It was fine. We remained until the afterpiece, and heard him in his last legs. Lovely day and night.

Wednesday, 9th. Snowed during forenoon, but melted before night. We remained at home in the evening. Nothing special going on.

Thursday, 10th. At the Office in the morning and until 3, P.M. At home balance of day, and evening. Mr. Davis spoke in the Senate to-day: made one of the best efforts of the session.

Friday, 11th. Mr. Hunter delivered an able speech in the Senate to-day.

Saturday, 12th. Mr. Seward delivered one of his Delphic Oracle speeches to-day—satisfied no one. There never has been such a crowd in the galleries as assembled there to-day. Several hundred persons came over on the morning Baltimore train to hear him. Cousins Clement and Virginia, and Lieut. Nelson, of the Navy, took dinner with us. We had an excellent dinner, and everything went off well. Anita played and sang some of her prettiest pieces after dinner. Cousin Clement went to a Senatorial Caucus after leaving us. Cousin Jeannie and I went to the theater and heard Hackett as "Colonel Nimrod Wildfire" in "The Wild Kentuckian of 1815," and in "Monsieur Mallet": he was very fine in both.

Sunday, 13th. Anita, Mary and I went to St. Matthew's Church in the forenoon: remained at home remainder of day and evening. Clear and cold — the coldest day I have felt this winter, I think.

Monday, 14th. At the Office until 3, P.M. I walked down to see Lt. Talbot in the afternoon. Very bad day: snow in the morning, and sleet at night. Anita was quite sick at night — she and Mary eat [sic] snow during the day, which gave her cold. Lt. Hall, and Mr. Hayne from South Carolina, arrived here from Charleston to-day, the former from Maj. Anderson's command, and the latter from his State, on a mission to President Buchanan.

Tuesday, 15th. In the evening I went to see Cousin Clement and Cousin Jeannie, and called by to see Mrs. McCormick: Cousin Jeannie and her friends at Brown's, were all going to the first Levee of the Season at the President's. Nannie Nells and her cousin have also gone. Rain and slush all day and at night.

Wednesday, 16th. Dined at Capt. Palmer's, Top. Engrs., at six P.M. Mr. Archibald Campbell, formerly of the Army, late Chief Clerk of the War Dept., and now Commissioner of the U.S. to define our North Western boundary, was the honored guest. Col. Lay, Capt. Flanklin, Capt. Humphreys, Capt. M.L. Smith and myself, with Mr. Hull Adams, were the company. Capt. and Mrs. Palmer presided with much dignity, and we spent a most delightful evening.

Thursday, 17th. I called to see Macfeely and his wife in the evening—saw Mac, but the madam had gone on a visit to Alexandria. I afterwards called at Mr. Davis', and spent an hour or so—met Gov. and Mrs. Fitzpatrick, Mr. and Mrs. Yulee, Mrs. Riggs and Dr. Smith there. Found Capt. and Mrs. Maynadier, with Henry and his wife at my house, when I returned.

Friday, 18th. Mild and wet all day and all night. I remained at home all the afternoon and evening.

Saturday, 19th. Anita, Mary and I spent the evening at Dr. Smith's, after making some other visits in the afternoon.

Sunday, 20th. We went to St. Aloisius church in the morning, and remained at home the balance of the day.

Monday, 21st. We went to the theater at night, and heard Jefferson in our "American Cousin." Cousin Jeannie sat with us. There was a very large audience.

Tuesday, 22nd. Nothing special going on.

Wednesday, 23rd. I went to Baltimore in the afternoon—took tea at Col. Van Nesse's, went with Col. Brush to see Mr. Cain, the Chief of Police, in regard to a rumored attack on Harper's

Ferry. Spent an hour or two at Dr. Jarvis'. Went to Barnum's, took tea, and went to bed.

Thursday, 24th. Returned to Washington in the morning. Very bad day—rain and snow. W.T. Magruder and his wife came over in the same train with me. I spent the evening with Cousin Jeannie, after calling a little while at Mr. McCormick's. Cousin Clement was very unwell to-night, with asthma.

Friday, 25th. Walked down the avenue after dinner, and remained at home during the evening. Cloudy and damp to-day.

Saturday, 26th. Snowed all day. Remained at home in the afternoon and evening. Hazen called in a little while after tea.

Sunday, 27th. I went to Mr. Pyne's church (Episcopal) and heard a Clergyman from Ireland on the subject of a bible society for the translation of the bible into Irish. Anita went to St. Matthews. After dinner we all went to Brown's to see Cousin Clement and Cousin Jeannie. We took Edward with us. Very mild and delightful to-day, although there is two or three inches of snow on the ground. There were a good many sleighs out during the day.

Monday, 28th. I was at the Office as usual. In the afternoon I walked down the avenue, and remained at home in the evening. Pleasant day—snow melting. Dr. and Mrs. Smith, and Miss Smith, came in and sat an hour or so after tea.

Tuesday 29th. Mary and I walked down the avenue after dinner. I remained at home in the evening.

<u>*Wednesday, 30th.*</u> Anita, Mary and I went to Col. Craig's after tea, but the ladies were out: we then stepped over to Capt. Jordan's and sat a while, although Mrs. Jordan was away.

<u>*Thursday, 31st.*</u> We all went to a hop at Brown's in the evening. Cousin Clement was suffering from asthma, but Cousin Jeannie managed to get down stairs in time for supper. The hop passed off very agreeably.

My pay, Col. Andrews, was $157.60, and my commutation, Capt. Miller, was $46.00. Anita's rents amounted to $100.00. Our income, therefore, was $303.60. Our expenses were $270.90. Our income exceeded our expenses by $32.69.

February, 1861.

Friday, 1st. I was at my Office as usual. In the evening, I walked down to see Cousin Clement. I met there Commander Page and Lt. Nelson, of the Navy. Mr. Judge, the Commissioner from Alabama, and Mr. Hayne, the Commissioner from South Carolina. Anita has headache to-day. Rained in the afternoon and evening. Foggy.

Saturday, 2nd. W.E. Jones took dinner with us to-day. I regret to notice in the papers the death of poor Ben Forsythe, a classmate and main friend of mine: he was found dead in his bed at Port Jervis, N.Y., yesterday morning. Softening of the brain was his disease, I believe. Snow melting, drizzly, and foggy to-day. A salute of thirty four guns was fired from the Armory grounds in this City to-day, in honor of the admission of Kansas into the union. Fry, in command of Magruder's battery, fired the Salute.

Sunday, 3rd. We went to St. Aloisius' in the morning, and heard Father McGuire. Cloudy and damp all day. In the evening we went to Brown's and spent an hour or two with Cousins Jeannie and Clement. Quite cool when we returned home.

<u>*Monday, 4th.*</u> Snowed last night, but melted during to-day. I visited some Officers in the afternoon.

<u>*Tuesday, 5th.*</u> Went to see Cousin Clement and Cousin Jeannie: found them packing up to leave.

<u>*Wednesday, 6th.*</u> Cousin Clement went to Petersburg to-day, to spend a few days with Cousin Thomas Withers. Cousin Jeannie went to Baltimore in the morning, and returned to our house in the evening.

<u>*Thursday, 7th.*</u> I was ordered to Texas to-day, but got the order changed, and Lt. Collins was sent in stead. Bitter cold to-day, and to-night. Very windy.

<u>*Friday, 8th.*</u> Very, very cold all day and night. We remained at home all day and at night.

<u>*Saturday, 9th.*</u> Anita, Mary, Cousin Jeannie and Mr. Judge, the Commissioner from the "Commonwealth" of Alabama, went to the reception at the President's to-day.

<u>*Sunday, 10th.*</u> Anita and Mary went to church. I went to the office a short time, and opened the mail. Mr. Judge dined with us to-day.

<u>*Monday, 11th.*</u> We all went to the theater at night, and saw Miss Charlotte Cushman as Queen Catherine, in Henry the Eighth.

Tuesday, 12th. We were sorry to part with Cousin Jeannie, who left us this afternoon. She seemed to regret leaving very much: she had many visitors, even up to the time of her departure. Mary, Anita and I went to hear Miss Cushman in the evening—she appeared as Meg Merriles.

Wednesday, 13th. Mary and I went to hear Miss Cushman as Lady Macbeth—Anita stayed at home. The votes for President and Vice President were counted to-day.

Thursday, 14th. This, St. Valentine's day, has been a very quiet one with us. Mrs. McCormick called in the afternoon, and Judge Hughes at night. Anita has had sick headache all day. Rained at night. The weather has been very mild for a week past.

Friday, 15th. Rained to-day. Nothing going on. I visited at Capt. Palmer's after tea. We changed cooks to-day.

Saturday, 16th. Nothing going on of a very special character. Lt. Washington, Aid-de-Camp to Genl. Twiggs, arrived here with dispatches from Texas this morning. I went with him to see Genl. Scott, and Maj. Townsend. Rained in the afternoon.

Sunday, 17th. Washington and I went to St. Aloisius, and Anita went to St. Matthew's church in the morning—Mary remained at home. Washington took dinner with us: — After tea, he and I went over and saw Mr. Gwin.

Monday, 18th. Nothing special going on.

Tuesday, 22nd. Washington left here for Texas yesterday. I am thirty-four years of age to-day, and my little boy is eleven months old. To-day is a holyday, and the citizen soldiery turned out—the regulars were to have paraded, but the order was countermanded. Beautiful day. We all went out to see the crowd.

Saturday, 23rd. Mr. Lincoln, the President elect, who was expected here in the afternoon, reached here early this morning: he called, with Mr. Seward, to see Genl. Scott and Mr. Buchanan. Mrs. McCormick went over to Annapolis to-day. I made some visits in the evening. Rained in the afternoon.

Sunday, 24th. Anita, Mary and I went to St. Matthew's Church in the morning, and heard a beautifully eloquent sermon by the Rev. Father Clarke, a native of this City. In the evening I walked down to Willard's, and saw Mrs. McLean a little while. Lovely moonlight night—just a cool enough to be agreeable. Anita is not well to-night.

Monday, 25th. Lovely day. Nothing special going on. I walked down the avenue after dinner.

Tuesday, 26th. Anita, Mary and I visited some in the afternoon, and spent the evening at Mrs. Gwin's: we had a most charming evening. Mrs. Gwin, Miss Lucy, and her younger sister and Mrs. Browne, with us, were the persons present. Beautiful day and night.

Wednesday, 27th. Fine day. Anita and Mary, with Edward and Charlotte, went to the Capitol, and spent some time to-day: Anita and I walked down to Capt. Garesché's after dinner, to inquire after his little child that has been very sick for several days past. We all feel elated to-day, because of a report that the peace conference, under the influence of Mr. Lincoln, has come to an amicable agreement about the settlement of our national troubles.

Thursday, 28th. Beautiful day—very mild. We all feel well, as there seems to be some hopes of the preservation of the Union. Anita and Mary went visiting to-day. I walked down to see Capt. Garesché after dinner, to ascertain if there was any way in which I could serve him, or in which Mary and Anita could assist his wife—they lost their youngest child this morning, and of course are greatly afflicted.

My pay, Col. Andrews, was $151.30: My commutation, Capt. Miller, was $46.00. Anita's rents amounted to $90.00. Our income, therefore, amounted to $287.30. Our expenses were $212.75. Our income exceeded our expenses by $74.55.

March, 1861.

Friday, 1st. Beautiful day—March has come in like a lamb. I walked down the Avenue after dinner, and took Anita to Church after tea. Billy Beall, who has just arrived here, called to see us while we were at Church—Mary entertained him and his nephew, young Abadie, for half an hour or so. The following Order was issued to-day; vis:

War Department
Adjt. Genl's. Office,

Genl. Orders No. 5.   Washington, March 1, 1861.

　　The following order is published for the information of the army:

　　　　　　War Department, March 1, 1861.

　　By the direction of the President of the United States it is ordered that Brigadier General David E. Twiggs, Major General by Brevet, be, and is hereby, dismissed from the Army of the United States, for his treachery to the flag of his country, in having surrendered, on the 18th. of February, 1861, on the demand of the authorities of Texas, the military posts and other property of the United States in his department, and under his charge.

(Signed) J. Holt
Secretary of War.

By Order of the Secretary of War.

(Signed) S. Cooper,

Adjutant Genl.

Saturday, 2nd. I was very busy to-day. A number of the Officers of the Army, Genl. Scott, Genl. Wool, Genl. Totten and others, called to say farewell to President Buchanan and Secretary Holt in succession—both of them made very pretty and affecting speeches: Genl. Scott spoke very feelingly on behalf of the Army. Anita and Mary called at Mrs. Douglas' to-day, and we all subsequently went to call on Billy Beall's Sister and Niece. Very warm to-day—disagreeably so. I walked down the avenue after dinner. In the evening Anita, Mary and I went to the Capitol and entered the Senate chamber—we heard a debate by Senators Pugh (Ohio), Baker (Oregon), Simmons (N. Jersey) and others on the Peace Conference measures. There was a great crowd of ladies and gentlemen in the galleries. We saw the U.S. Flag floating over the Capitol: long may it continue to do so.

Sunday, 3rd. We went to St. Aloisius Church in the morning. Mrs. Cochrane, her daughter, Billy Beall and young Abadie took dinner with us. In the afternoon Anita, Mary and I took a walk—delightful weather. We had no fire all day, nor in the evening.

Monday, 4th. Fine day—a little windy. I was kept at the Office until near one O'Clock, copying some of Major Anderson's letters for Mr. Holt, and finishing up some other business which it was desirable to have closed at once. Anita, Mary, Mrs. Cochrane, and her daughter, under the escort of Billy

Beall and young Abadie, went down to the Kirkwood House, and had a fine view of the Presidential Cortege as it passed down the Avenue: I got down in time to see the procession on its way back from the Capitol to the White House after the completion of the inaugural ceremonies. Mr. Lincoln's inaugural address will be variously interpreted according to the hopes and fears of the different readers of it: for myself, I see much in it to encourage the hope of a conciliatory course on the part of the President. There was no enthusiasm to-day.

Tuesday, 5th. Very windy, quite cold, and altogether disagreeable. Anita, Mary, Mrs. Cochrane, her daughter and Billy Beall went to the Patent Office, notwithstanding the impropitiousness of the day.

Wednesday, 6th. I received a letter from Cousin Withers Clay, and one from Aunt Clay, this morning, urging me to resign my commission in the Army at once. I went to see Bell at Mr. McCormick's in the evening: he, and all my friends in the Army, oppose my resigning. Pleasant day.

Thursday, 7th. I resigned my Commission in the Army of the United States to-day, and it was accepted by the President, to take effect the first of March, 1861. Colonel Samuel Cooper Adjutant General, U.S.A., also resigned, and his resignation was accepted to take effect March 7th, 1861. Dr. Smith called in the evening—I subsequently walked down to see Billy Beall at the Kirkwood House—he was out. Beautiful day. A great many of my friends were in the Office to see me to-day, to advise me to wait a while before resigning.

Friday, 8th. Anita and Mary visited most of the day. I wrote several letters at the Office. A great many persons called to express their regrets at our having determined to leave the City.

Saturday, 9th. Very bad day: rained hard until the afternoon. I packed my books to-day, and Anita packed some of her clothes. Several of our friends came in to see us at night: some remained very late.

Sunday, 10th. We went to St. Aloisius' church in the morning. Billy Beall took dinner with us. Cloudy and cool. Capt. and Mrs. McLean called in the afternoon.

Monday, 11th. I was busy all day getting ready to move. A good many of our friends called to see us during the day and evening. Beautiful day and night. The withdrawal of the troops from Fort Sumter appears to have been definitively set-tled upon—this certainly must have a most soothing effect upon the Southern people. When the *people* come to be heard, as eventually must be the case, the rebellion, I think, will be put down.

Tuesday, 12th. Cloudy in the morning. Busy all day getting ready to start. Many friends called to see us in the evening.

Wednesday, 13th.-Thursday, 14th., Friday, 15th. We were travel-ing the above days from Washington, D.C., to Huntsville, Alabama: reaching the latter place about 1, P.M. on Friday. Mary went to Uncle LeVert's, and Anita and I went to Aunt Clay's—Uncle Clay was at the plantation.

<u>*Sunday, 31st.*</u> We have spent the past 16 days with our relatives in Huntsville: we have had an agreeable visit.

I drew pay from the 17th. (the date of my appointment), until the 31st. inclusive, which amounted to ($79.00) seventy nine dollars. Anita's rents amounted to $60.00.
Our income, therefore, was $139.00.
Our expenses were $313.15.
Our expenses exceeded our income, by $174.15.

April, 1861.

Anita and I left Huntsville on the 1st., and reached Montgomery on the 3rd., from which time until the end of the month I continued on duty in the Adjutant General's Office. We remained at the Exchange Hotel until the 29th., when we secured lodgings at Mrs. Ponder's, on the hill: the madam is a rich widow, who took us at the insistence of several mutual friends. Many important events have transpired during this month which I ought to have recorded, but which, having failed to notice as they occurred, I do not now recollect in their order, and so omit mention of all except the bombardment and reduction of Fort Sumter, and the secession of Virginia from the U.S. Government.

Anita: March - April, 1861. We left Washington on the 13th. for Huntsville, where we spent two weeks. About April the 8th. the C— accepted the same position in the Confederate Army which he had in the old one.

My pay for April was $158.00, and my Commutation from the 3rd. until the 30th., inclusive, was $36.39. Anita's rents amounted to $57.50. Our income, therefore, was $251.89. Our expenses were, $440.79.

Our expenses exceeded our income, by $188.90.
We paid this month $174.54 of last and this year's expenses—
for the taxes for the year, cleaning ditches, and four months
commissions for collecting this year.

May, 1861.

Tuesday, 14th. Anita and I are getting on well at Mrs. Ponder's. The weather is becoming quite warm, and mosquitoes begin to abound. Genl. Cooper and I are in charge of the Adjt. Genl's. Department: Lt. Col. Deas and Maj. Clay both having been ordered to Virginia. President Davis, and Mrs. Davis, went to Pensacola to-day. Capt. Josselyn, Capt. Shaaff and Miss Saunders spent the evening with us. Edward is not well to-day.

Wednesday, 15th. Quite cool in the morning.

Friday, 17th. Anita and I attended a reception at Mr. Toombs' in the evening, which was a most agreeable reunion. We saw the vice President, (Mr. Stephens), Mr. Rives from Va., and other men of eminence. Mr. and Mrs. Wigfall (Texas), Mr. and Mrs. and Miss Memminger, (S.C.), Gov. and Mrs. Fitzpatrick, (Ala.), Mrs. Pope Walker, Miss Howell, (sister of Mrs. Davis) and many others, were present. We had refreshments. My wife was as handsomely dressed, and as handsome, as the handsomest. We remained from nine until half after ten O'Clock, P.M. Weather very agreeable indeed.

<u>*Sunday, 19th.*</u> Genl. Cooper, Lt. Groner and I, were kept at work in the Office all the morning. Rained hard from eleven, A.M., until one P.M. Maj. Beall and Mr. Calvert called to see us late in the afternoon.

<u>*Monday, 20th.*</u> Anita and I called to see Mrs. Davis after tea. We met Mr. Rives and Mrs. R.M.T. Hunter, of Va., and Mr. and Mrs. Wall, of Texas. Pleasant weather.

<u>*Tuesday, 21st.*</u> Our little boy has not been well for three weeks past—yesterday I got a homeopathic physician to call and see him, and he is better to-day. I called at the President's about two, P.M: this is to be Mrs. Davis' last reception, for the present, I understand. Maj. Beall and Mrs. Wall called to see Anita in the evening.

<u>*Wednesday, 22nd.*</u> Quite cool this morning; so much so that we had a little fire in our room before breakfast.

<u>*Wednesday, 29th.*</u> During the past week Congress has adjourned, and we have all packed up for a move to Richmond, Virginia, in pursuance of a resolution which was passed prior to the adjournment (removing the seat of Government to the latter place). Many have gone already, and Anita and I are to leave in the morning, at eight O'Clock. Alexandria, Va., has been occupied, during the past week, by troops from Washington City.

<u>*Thursday, 30th.*</u> We left Montgomery for Richmond early in the morning. The baby stood the day's travel very well.

<u>*Anita: April-May*</u>. *We moved to Mrs. Ponder 29th. April—and left for Richmond where the seat of Government was changed to on the 30th. May.*

My pay this month was $158.00, and my commutation $30.00, both paid by Maj. J.L. Calhoun. My transportation from Montgomery, Alabama, to Richmond, Virginia, was $87.60, paid by Major Larkin Smith, Asst. Qr. Master at the latter place.

June, 1861.

Anita: June 1st. *We arrived in Richmond on the 2ond of the month and stopped at the Spotswood, the same place where President Davis and family stayed.*

We moved to Mrs. Duval's on 5th. We are very much pleased with the house and boarders.

Edward walked for the first time on the 8th. of June. The Capt. and myself were exceedingly delighted to see him, he was just fourteen months and half old when he made his first attempt.

June 15th. *The anniversary of our marriage. We were married two years today, and Eddie was christened a year ago.*

We took a ride out to the Camps yesterday to see Mrs. Rodes, but she had gone to Lynchburg. Mrs. Duval and her little boy went with us. Eddie looked mighty sweet and pretty with his hat trimmed with blue. In the evening we went round to the Exchange to see Mrs. James Purcell.

Sunday, 16th. During the past two weeks (we arrived here just two weeks ago to-day) I have been hard at work in the Office. Great numbers of troops have arrived here from the South.

On Monday last, the 10th., an engagement took place between the U.S. and the Confederate States forces at Bethel Church near Yorktown, in which the latter utterly routed the former, although the latter had only 1,200 men whilst the former are reported to have had 4,000. It is reported that our loss was only one killed, and half a dozen wounded, whilst theirs was 225 killed, and great numbers wounded: they acknowledge to having lost 30 killed and about a hundred wounded. I have been kept so busy with my Official duties lately that I have neglected almost all others—the keeping up of my journal amongst the rest; and that, too, at a time when I ought to have written it out most regularly and carefully. Last Thursday was a fast day, on the recommendation of President Davis: we heard the Bishop of Charleston preach, and afterward called to see him, and Bishop McGill.

Anita: June 21st. This was the hottest and most oppressive night I ever felt, we could not go to sleep for a long time. Eddie was very restless. About three O'clock a terrible storm came up, I became very much frightened. I thought we were all going to be destroyed. The house shook awfully.

June 22nd. Edward was 15 months old today, he is better now than I have seen him for months, he has another tooth nearly through.

Sunday, 23rd. I have been kept very busy at the Office during the past week: the weather has been hot. Anita went to early Mass this morning, and I went to St. Paul's (Episcopal) Church at eleven O'Clock. Edward is getting on finely—he has eight teeth.

Anita: June 23rd. I arose this morning at half past five, took a bath, and went to Church at half past six. I felt **so** very weak that I thought I would certainly faint. Last night Captain Jones came 15 miles Just to see the Captain, he went to see Mrs. Davis.

Monday, 24th. A number of Captains and Lieutenants of some North Alabama Companies which are to form a Regiment, sent in a written petition to the President to-day, to have me appointed their Colonel: I sent the petition to the Secretary of War myself. These gentlemen have been verbally endeavoring to accomplish the same object for more than a week past.

Saturday, 29th. Another petition from the gentlemen above-mentioned, and to the same effect, was taken to the President to-day by Genl. O'Neal (the Major of the Regiment).

We have had nothing especially interesting to occur this week.

Mr. Lamar, from Mississippi, the Lt. Col. of Col. Mott's 19th. Miss. Regiment, had a stroke of Apoplexy or paralysis to-night, in camp, from which it is feared he cannot recover.

Sunday, 30th. Anita and I went to Church in the forenoon: we were kept in by rain sometime after services ended. Forney got here last night, and part of his Regiment will be here to-day: the remainder will arrive this week.

My pay this month was $155.00, and my Commutation $30.00, both paid by Major Larkin Smith Qr. Mr.

July, 1861.

Anita: July [4th.] The fourth was celebrated here in a very quiet way. Eddie was taken sick suddenly last night about twelve O'clock, he suffered very much, we were up with him all night. The next morning we called Dr. Brewer to see him, who stays in the house, he got better by the afternoon. Mrs. Duval was exceedingly kind, she nursed him nearly all day.

July 6th. I was sick with the headache nearly all day, by night I got worse. I am crocheting Eddie a sack, the first I ever did.

Sunday, July 7th. The Captain and myself went to Church, Bishop McGill preached. Edward is not very well today. After Church I wrote to my Mother.

Monday, July 8th. The Bishop came to see me and inquired whether I was going out to the Amelia Springs. The baby is still sick.

Wednesday, 10th. One week ago, last night, we noticed a very large and distinct comet located in the North West—it was about as large and distinct as any I have ever seen save one. It was still visible last night. The weather has been very warm for a week past, and our dear little boy has been sick, cutting teeth, during the same time. The day before yesterday I got a

Dentist to pull out a piece of the root of one of my jaw teeth—
it had been gradually working its way to the surface for three
years.

Anita: Wednesday, 10th. Eddie was very ill all day, I packed my
trunk to go to the Springs with him. In the Afternoon Mrs. Toombs
and Mrs. Brown called to see me. Mrs. T. was exceedingly kind, of-
fered to come and sit up with Eddie at night. Miss Lee and Mrs.
Warrick also called. I sent Eddie round to the Square, he couldn't
even hold his little head up.

Thursday, July 11th. We had a terrible night last night. My baby
was extremely ill, nauseated so much that we thought he could not
possibly stand it. Mrs. Govan came up about 2 O'clock hearing him
cry so pitifully. Dr. Brewer was waked up to see him, and ordered a
black blister to be put on him for two hours and half, that seemed to
relieve him more than anything else.

About 10 O'clock Dr. Conway was called in to see him, he told me
Eddie was a very sick child but still there was nothing alarming in
his symptoms.

Friday, July 12th. The baby still quite ill. Mrs. Pulaski was kind
enough to ask us out to her country place. We promised to go out
next week.

Sunday, July 14th. Eddie did not spend a good night, seemed to be
in pain all the time, this morning I did not go to Church, stayed at
home with Eddie all day. Mrs. Johnston and McLane called on me
yesterday.

<u>*On Thursday, July 18th.*</u> *The Captain had to call in Dr. Conway again, for we thought little Eddie sicker and very feeble. On Friday the darling got very low, by evening we could not warm his little feet and hands. I was all ready and packed yesterday (deed have been for the last week) to go out to the country, mountains, or in any direction that could benefit my Angel, but the Physicians objected to my going. I suppose they knew all the time that my babe was too ill.*

Friday afternoon such a change took place that I had very little or no hope of the baby's recovery.

*Mrs. Dr. Wait was kind enough to send me round her carriage. Dr. Conway was in at the time, so he told us to take Edie out to drive, it could [not] hurt him. I went with an **aching, agonizing** heart, expecting every moment for my child to go off. I **never shall forget** that ride and that evening as long as I live. I weeped all the time.*

*That night Dr. C. ordered us to give him 20 drops of Paregoric as a last resort or remedy, to produce sleep. Mrs. Duval, who was a kind, good friend to us all during his sickness, assisted us in nursing that his last night in this world of sorrows and troubles. My own precious suffered terribly all night, he could not get any rest for more than 10 minutes at a time. I could scarcely control myself, my **anxiety** and **pain** of **mind** and **heart** were terrible.*

<u>*Saturday, July 20th.*</u> *My own babe was gradually and quietly fading away, like a little Angel that he was, travelling to his Heavenly Home, where no pain, sickness, or sorrow will ever reach him.*

Bishop McGill came just a few moments before my babe departed, which was about three O'clock in the afternoon. The Bishop tried to comfort and console us, but it was difficult at that time of intense grief and anguish of heart. I felt as if they were tearing my soul from my body. He was layed out in the little room.

<u>Saturday, 20th.</u> After suffering with sick stomach and purging bowels since the night of the 4th., Inst., our dear Angel Baby, Eddy, quietly breathed his last, at three O'Clock this afternoon. Bishop McGill, my wife and I, with poor old Charlotte, were with him when he died. The blessed Angel is in Heaven: We are bereft, indeed. Dr. Brewer, Asst. Surg. C.S. Army, and Dr. Conway, Professor in the Richmond Medical College, did all that science could do; and Mrs. Duval, her sister Mrs. Govan, and Miss Susan Duval, helped my wife, myself, and Charlotte, to nurse him tenderly, but all to no avail. God wished him to be at home, and therefore took him to Heaven.

<u>Anita:</u> *Col. Chilton and [sic] watched that night. The next day he was put in the coffin, buried on Sunday afternoon, the day the Grand battle at Manassas was fought. The Bishop read the Funeral Service in the parlour, and made a beautiful address, I did not go down but the ladies told me. The parlour was crowded with ladies and gentlemen, Mrs. President Davis, Mrs. Johnston, Mrs. Wigfall, and McLean had the politeness to attend. My own was layed in the Bishop's Vault, so as to take him home with us when we return.*

That same Sunday night The Captain took me round to Mrs. Nelson's, I went stait up to bed. We spent a whole week there, with exception of one day and night that we spent at Mr. Williams'. Mrs. Nelson and all the ladies were exceedingly kind to us.

Sunday, 21st. Our Angel Boy was put away to rest just before the sun went down. At 5 O'Clock, P.M., Bishop McGill read the prayers of the Church for the burial of children, in the parlor at Mrs. Duval's, and afterward made a most beautiful discourse on the subject of infant baptism. My wife was not present. I was down stairs. Mrs. President Davis, Mrs. Genl. Johnston, Mrs. Maj. McLean, Mrs. Major Blair, Mrs. Capt. Williams, the ladies and gentlemen at our house, and a few other friends were in attendance. Lovely day. Col. Chilton, Captain Williams, Mr. Duval, and Mr. Branch, were the pall bearers. Col. Chilton and Captain Deshler sat up with our infant's body last night. My wife and I went up to Mrs. Nelson's after tea, and remained all night.

At night we learned that this sacred day to all, to us doubly so, has been the occasion of the greatest battle ever fought on this continent, and in which the Southern forces have been entirely successful. President Davis was on the field at Manassas Junction, Va., in the afternoon. About 55,000 men of the Northern Army fought about 35,000 of the Southern Army from early morn until near nightfall, when the former were utterly routed. Night closed in on their full retreat, and our eager pursuit.

Anita: Sunday, July the 28th. We went to late Mass, I was in deep black. The Bishop gave a beautiful Sermon.

The Southern Congress met here the day that my own darling died.

Wednesday, 31st. My wife and I spent a week at Mrs. Nelson's, and then returned home, where we have since remained.

Great numbers of sick, wounded, and prisoners, from the North, and numbers of our sick and wounded have been brought down, and cared for in various hospitals and private houses in this city.

My pay, Maj. Larkin Smith, was $158.00, and my Commutation, the same gentleman, was $30.00, for the month.

August, 1861.

<u>Thursday, 1st.</u> Brother Fred, who arrived in the City last night, came to see us to-day!!

Anita: August 1st. Fred arrived here from Louisiana today. Dear Aunt Mollie sent Eddie a bottle of blackberry cordial, not having heard of his death.

<u>Sunday, 4th.</u> Very warm. Anita and I went to church in the morning, and heard an excellent sermon from Bishop McGill.

<u>Friday, 9th.</u> I have been kept very busy at the Office all this week. The weather has been oppressively warm. Anita has been feeble, and had headache yesterday—she is better to-day. We had a heavy rain towards nightfall. Fred received orders yesterday, and reported to Genl. Winder to-day for duty—he is assigned to duty with the guard for the Yankee Prisoners.

<u>Anita: Sunday, August 11th.</u> The Captain and myself went to St. Peter's Church. We had a fine sermon by Bishop McGill "On Charity." After Church we walked round to Mr. John Purcell's for a little while returned home and read a letter from Angel. How strange things happen in this world. Concion's little girl was born on the

day that my Angel Boy was buried. I felt miserable the rest of the day, in fact all the time I have felt loneliness and sadness.

<u>August 17th</u>. We received a sweet letter from Sister Sue. We both wept when we read her comforting words. Fred is on guard duty down at the prison.

<u>Sunday, August 18th.</u> The Captain and myself went to Church at ten O'clock. A new and Young Priest preached a pretty good Sermon but timidly and hurriedly.

<u>On Thursday the 22nd.</u> The Captain and myself went round to the Bishop's this morning a little while to try and get the key of the Vault, he directed us to go to the Sexton. In the Afternoon the Captain, Charlotte and myself went out to the cemetery, it is a desolate looking place where my babe is buried, but I hope we will soon take him home.

<u>Saturday 24th.</u> The Captain took me over to Petersburg. We left here at three O'clock. Cousin Tom and his nephew Mr. Adams went to the cars to meet us. We remained all the next day. Mrs. Hinton, quite a nice lady, called round for me to go to church with her. I took a nice long drive with Mr. Adams in the Afternoon. Aunt Walker came to see me, and took tea with us, she seems to be a sterling woman.

<u>Anita: Monday morning 26th.</u> We arose at three O'clock and left on the cars for Richmond at half past four. In the afternoon Capt. and Mrs. Williams took us to drive, we spent the evening there. I went round to the Office with the Captain. A soldier died at Mrs. Nelson's.

Monday, 26th. Anita and I went over to Petersburg Saturday afternoon, and returned early this morning. We stayed at Cousin Tom Withers', and had a most delightful visit. We saw Aunt Dolly Walker, Cousin Tom Adams, and his sister, Mrs. Boggs. The weather has been much cooler for ten days past. I am kept very busy, every day.

Tuesday 27th. I went to see Mrs. Chilton. After Tea my Husband went to the Office. Capt. Myers, his wife and myself to Pizzini's.

Wednesday 28th. We went round to our friend Mrs. Nelson's to take Tea, she gave me some yarn to nit [sic] socks for the soldiers.

Saturday, 31st. Congress to-day fixed the rank of the Generals in the Army of the Confederate States as follows:
    Samuel Cooper.
    Albert S. Johnston.
    Robert E. Lee
    Joseph E. Johnston.
    G.T. Beauregard.

Anita: Saturday, August 31st. I got up with a head ache. Mrs. Brewer and myself went to Market and bought some peaches. I was nitting nearly all day, making socks for the soldiers. In the afternoon I went to Confession to Bishop McGill. The Captain walked back from Church with me.

My pay was $158.00, and my Commutation $30.00, both paid by Maj. Larkin Smith.

September, 1861.

Anita: Tuesday, September 3rd. I went to Mrs. Nelson's in the morning, took my nitting and remained for about three hours. I met Mrs. Dr. Wayt there, she invited to Tea the next evening. Captain and Mrs. Williams called in the evening to see us, there was quite an excitement, a poor old Negro man was robbed and beaten on the street, he made a great noise. The Gentlemen ran to his assistance.

Saturday, September 7th. All day at home. In the evening Captain Myers took his wife, Mrs. Brewer and myself to Pizzinis to get some ice cream. My Husband did not come until after eleven, he was kept on bus— —with Gen. Johnston.

Thursday, September 12th. The Captain took me in a carriage down to the depot at half past seven. Mrs. Williams and her little gang were Just in time. Mr. Seldon's carriage was waiting for us.

We spent a delightful time in the country. On Saturday afternoon the 14th. My Husband and Captain Williams went out to see us, they remained there until Sunday afternoon. In the morning they went to the Presbyterian country Church, Mr. Converse preached. We spent Monday 16th. at Mrs. Pollard's.

On Tuesday about ten we left Mr. Seldon's for the depot, arrived there at twelve, and had to wait for the cars until four in the evening. The Captain was at the depot with a carriage. Mrs. Col. Chilton called on me the same day that I returned. I found Captain and Mrs. Myers had gone home.

On Wednesday 18th. Mrs. Col. Myers called on me. In the afternoon the Captain and myself went to call on Mrs. Gen. Cooper—and Mrs. Greenhow—

Sunday, September 22nd. My babe would have been one year and half old today. The Captain and myself went to Church at ten O'clock. Bishop McGill preached a beautiful Sermon on the "forgiveness of sins" or Confession. In the Afternoon I went to Vespers and to see Mrs. Stewart. My Husband walked back home with me.

Thursday 26th. ... I leave for Petersburg this afternoon.

Saturday, September 28th. I have had a very pleasant time here. Cousin Celeste and myself dined at the Rev'd Mr. Gibson's. We met old Mrs. Wheat, we were quite amused at all the airs she put on. The Captain came over to see us.

Sunday, September 29th. The Captain and myself went to the Catholic Church with Mr. Mrs. Hinton. After Church time about 2 O'clock Cousin Lawson came over from Lynchburg. We all dined together. On Monday the Captain returned to Richmond. We took a long walk in the afternoon, went to see Aunt Walker.

My pay this month was $158.00, and my Commutation $30.00, both paid by Lt. Col. Larkin Smith.

October, 1861.

<u>Anita: Wednesday, October 2nd.</u> *Cousin Celeste and myself went out in the morning and made some calls. Poor old Charlotte sprained her wrist and had quite a severe fall. About diner time it was pouring down raining, I determined to leave for Richmond although they all begged me not to leave in such rain. Tom took me to the cars and got my tickets. To my very great disappointment and disgust when I reached the City the Captain was not there to meet me. I and Charlotte got into an Omnibus and came home, it was pouring down raining all the time. The Captain was Just a few minutes too late.*

<u>Sunday, October 13th.</u> *The Captain and myself went to Church. We had no Music again. We had a fine Sermon from the Bishop. The Capt. went to hear Mr. Duncan preach in the evening, and was much pleased.*

On Monday I took a walk in the morning, and went round to see Mrs. Ayres. In the evening Capt. and I went to call at the Spotswood on several ladies, Mrs. Johnston, Myers, and Guild. Oct. 14th. 1861,—and Mrs. Washington called to see us.

<u>On Tuesday 15th.</u> *I walked up to Hirsh's in the morning to buy some worstered, I met Mrs. Williams and Washington—as I*

returned I met with Mrs. Nelson and sister who had just called on me. Mrs. N. proposed that we should call on Mrs. President Davis as it was such a lovely day. I although much fatigued agreed to do so—we went up, but did not see the Madam, too much indisposed.

We were invited to Tea at Mrs. Wayt's but I had a sick head ache and could not go with my Husband. Mrs. Duval thoughtful and kind as ever came up to see me—Col. and Mrs. Beall called.

<u>Wednesday, October 16th.</u> I am better today. I went out for a little while. Dr. Leland wanted to see the Captain—Gen. as he called him. Mr. DeCoeniel came to see me about taking music lessons. The Captain took a ride after dinner.

<u>Sunday, October 20th.</u> This morning I went to Church alone, we had no Music nor Sermon, the Bishop I believe is away. We spent the evening at Mrs. Nelson's.

<u>Monday, October 21st.</u> We had a grand victory over the Yankees at Leesburg. Captain Evans commanded and behaved splendidly. I commenced to knit a Sontag for Cousin Celeste. I went out to see Mrs. Washington. In the afternoon Mrs. Dr. Wayt took me to drive. We saw the North Carolina Regiment of Calvary reviewed by the President.

<u>Tuesday 22nd.</u> We heard of the death of poor Gus, he died of typhoid fever. I commenced taking Music lessons from Mr. DeCoeniel. Miss Susan sits in the room.

Tuesday, October 29th. *I went out this morn to call on Mrs. Gen. Winder. I also called on Mrs. Washington, we gossiped a **good deal**. This morning I walked with the Capt. to the Office and back.*

Thursday, October 31st. *Mrs. Williams and her friend Miss Crenshaw called. I had bad head ache all day Friday, but I took my Music lesson, and was particularly stupid about it. I went to bed about 5 O'clock, it rained terribly all night long. All Saint's day, I went to Church.*

My pay this month was $158.00, and my Commutation $45.00, both paid by Lt. Col. Larkin Smith.

November, 1861.

Anita: Wednesday 13th. I went to the Dentist and had a tooth pulled out, Mrs. Duval was with me. In the evening we went to Mr. J. Purcell's and took Tea. I felt badly and nervous, came home right sick, went to bad and had high fever all night and next day. Dr. Brewer came to see me. I remained in bed for two days, missed one Music lesson.

Tuesday 19th. I took my Music lesson and finished taking the "Rocketts." The Captain is reading Oliver Twist to me.

Thursday 21st. I went to the Dentist, Dr. Wayt, this morning, and had 4 teeth plugged. Mrs. Wayt sent me an elegant lunch, which I did not eat until two O'clock.

Sunday 24th. We went to Church at eleven. Bishop McGill preached. After Ch— we went home with Mrs. James Purcell. We had a very nice dinner, but I did not enjoy it, for I suffered most violently with a head ache—they had to send me home in a carriage.

Thursday 28th. I went round to Dr. Wayt's this morning, he finished fixing my teeth and pulled out one. The Captain went to a concert that Mr. DeCorneil gave for the benefit of the Soldiers, I did not go for the evening was very damp and raining.

Saturday 30th. *I walked to the Office in the morning. In the afternoon the Captain was invited to a dinner party at Mr. Menard's, he did not return until half past ten O'clock. I went to Confession and walked home after dark with Charlotte.*

My pay this month was $158.00, and my Commutation $49.50, both paid by Lt. Col. Larkin Smith.

December, 1861.

Anita: Sunday 1st. of December. I did not sleep well last night. The Captain was sick all night. I got up at seven O'clock to go to Mass and communion. I remained at home in the evening.

Wednesday 4th. I went out immediately after breakfast and bought me a nice set of furs at $40. also some few little things for Charlotte. I called on Mrs. Dr. Moore and Joyns, and went to tell Mrs. Wash—goodbye. In the evening Captain and myself went to Mrs. Nelson's to spend the evening.

Thursday 5th. I took a Music lesson, and then took a walk on broad street— purchased some little worstereds and things. I stayed in my room all the evening.

Friday 6th. We went to see Mrs. Munford in the afternoon and from there we went to Mrs. James Purcell's to spend the evening. Mr. Cowarden was there, we had a very nice quiet evening.

Sunday the 8th. I went to Church at ten O'clock. Father Andrews preached a good Sermon. We walked up to Mr. John Purcell's to Tea, we met Mr. and Mrs. Cranz and Mr. Menard there.

Monday 9th. The Captain and myself made a few calls in the after-noon.

On Tuesday we were invited to the wedding, it did not come off, both lady and gentleman being under age they had to run off to North Carolina to get married.

<u>Wednesday 11th.</u> I took my lesson. I have a sore throat, and the Captain is complaining greatly.

<u>Saturday 14th.</u> I went out to pay some calls. I also went to see the young bride, Mrs. Reed, and Mrs. Menard. I took my Music lesson.

<u>Sunday 15th.</u> I went to Church at eleven, we had a poor sermon from a young priest. Returning I got caught at the Square gate and had a good deal of trouble in passing through. I had a good cry about it after I came home, did not go down to dinner, but went to bed with an awful headache. I suffered all night.

<u>Christmas Day, Wednesday, 25th.</u> We went to Church at 10 O'clock. Father McMullen preached a very good sermon. After Church we all went to Mr. John Purcell's and took a glass of egg-nog, and from there we went to see the Sisters, Mrs. Randolph took us ladies in her carriage. (The Stable of Bethlehem was beautiful.) The little Orphans sang for us. About five we walked up to Mr. Menard's to dine—we returned about nine.

On Thursday I walked out in the morning. In the evening we were invited to Mrs. Nelson's. We had a very pleasant time, the young ladies danced. Dr. Wayt played the violin, and amused us all greatly.

My pay this month was $158.00, and my Commutation $48.00, both paid by Lt. Col. Larkin Smith.

Anita and I spent Christmas eve at Mr. Maury's. We went to Church Christmas day, and dined at Mr. Maynard's. We spent the evening after Christmas at Mrs. Nelson's. Altogether we had as cheerful a time as we could have had under the circumstances.

In a letter dated December 30, 1861, Cowan's Auctions (which auctioned off this letter, among many others) reported that John Withers wrote to Col. Reuben Campbell, confirming that William H. Sanford was to be commissioned to the 7th North Carolina regiment. Further, according to Cowan's Auctions, "Withers concludes with sarcastic comments that would come to haunt Abraham Lincoln as Union commander-in-chief." Withers wrote, "We have nothing new here—everybody is in the same state of expecting of McClellan's advance that has existed these three months. G.W. Smith, Whiting, Beauregard, and Joe Johnston are all anxious for him to come on to Richmond as fast as he can."

January, 1862.

<u>Wednesday, 1st.</u> Anita and I walked up to see Mrs. Thos. G. Williams after church. I went to the President's Levee, the first general one he has given in Richmond. Mrs. Davis was not visible, her little child being only a few weeks old. The President and his Aid, Col. G.W.C. Lee, received us at the door of the middle room: we were there presented to Mrs. D.R. Jones, and Miss Howell, the former a relative of the President's first wife, and the latter the sister of his second wife. I called at a few other places.

<u>Anita: Wednesday, January 1st</u>. *New Year's day was a lovely day — quite mild but windy. We went to Church at 10 O'clock. Father Andrews preached. After Church Captain and myself walked up to see Mrs. Williams, she had been sick and was looking wretchedly — she made a nice egg-nog for us. From there The Capt. and Mrs. Williams walked with me to Mrs. Nelson's where I remained until they returned from the President's, who had a Reception. Crowds of people passed by. The band played some pretty airs.*

<u>Sunday, 5th.</u> To-day is my wife's twenty third birthday. We went to church, dined at home (Mrs. Duvall's) and had some cake and cherry bounce in our room after dinner: Dr. and Mrs. Brewer enjoyed the latter with us, and we sent some up to Mr.

and Mrs. Branch. The weather has been charming during the holidays, but it turned very cold yesterday and has been bitterly so to-day—sleeting occasionally.

I heard, a few days since, of the death of my dear Aunt Mary Woodson Withers, which took place at Huntsville, or rather near there, on the nineteenth of December, 1861. Thus in one year I lost my Angel Baby, my Cousin Augustine J. Withers, who was like a brother, and my dear Aunt, who was my mother in feeling and action after mother's death. God knows that 1861 was a sad year for me.

Anita: Sunday 5th. My birthday, I completed my 23rd. year today. The Capt. gave me a beautiful cake. We went to Church at eleven. I dressed finely for dinner, after which we invited Dr. and Mrs. Brewer to take a glass of wine and cake with us. Major Williams came round to see us. Poor Judge Hemphill is dead.

Thursday, 9th. The weather has been quite cold for a few days until last night when it moderated very much. We have a heavy atmosphere of fog and smoke to breathe to-night. A little rain fell last night, but to-night we have moonlight through the fog. There has been a dearth of news all this week.

Anita: Thursday, January 9. A gloomy rainy day, I stayed at home all day. I wrote to Mary McClelland. I took a singing lesson.

Friday 10th. I took a nice long walk after I got through practising—and went to the Office for the Captain. In the evening we sat in the parlour, Mrs. Abbott is to leave early tomorrow morning.

<u>Sunday, 12th.</u> I went to see Stevens in the morning, (W.H. Stevens, of the Engineers, a classmate of mine) who came down from Manassas a couple of days since, and is now sick at the Spotswood Hotel.

<u>Tuesday, 14th.</u> Genl. Cooper and Col. Deas went up to Manassas last evening. A considerable fall of snow occurred last night. Genls. Longstreet, Jones and Van Dorn are down from Manassas. Anita and I went to an entertainment at Dr. Wayt's in the evening—we took Mr. and Mrs. Duval in our carriage. I dined at Mr. John Purcell's and had a most agreeable time with a dozen other gentlemen.

<u>Anita: Tuesday 14th. January.</u> *I did not go out all day, it snowed heavily. We went to Mrs. Wayt's in the evening, we had to hire a carriage for it was hailing and sleeting. Mr. and Mrs. Duval went with me first to Mr. Purcell's to get the Captain who was dining there. I had a letter from Catarina.*

<u>Wednesday, 15th.</u> Rained to-day, making the walking very bad indeed. We had more quiet at the office to-day than is usual, no doubt owing to the state of the weather.

<u>Anita: Wednesday 15th.</u> *We had a very nice entertainment last evening, a delightful supper. I wore my purple dress, and my hair platted in front. I took a music lesson.*

<u>Thursday 16th.</u> *Raining all the time. I could not go out.*

<u>Friday 17th.</u> *I practised soon after breakfast as usual. Afterwards I dressed and walked to see Mrs. Northrope—it is dreadfully muddy.*

In the evening I dressed to go to Mrs. Nelson's, but it was raining. Cousin Edmund came to see us.

<u>Saturday 18th.</u> I took my lesson. I have just heard of the death of poor Ex-President Tyler.

I went up to Mrs. Brewer's room and commenced making me a large collar.

*<u>Sunday 19th.</u> We went Church and a good Sermon from Father Mc on marriage, in the Afternoon we went Mrs. Nelson's. We were surprised to see poor old Mrs. Grenhow **so very** lone—we remained there until after Tea.*

<u>Monday 20th.</u> I went around to see how Mrs. G. was getting along, much worse, they have been sitting up with her for several nights.

<u>Tuesday 21st. of January.</u> She died about nine O'clock in the morning, they all said it was really beautiful to hear the way she talked to her children.

<u>Tuesday, 21st.</u> Ex President John Tyler, who died a little after twelve O'Clock last Friday night, the 17th, or rather the morning of the 18th., was buried to-day: his remains were carried from the Capitol to St. Paul's Church, where the funeral sermon was preached by Right Rev. Bishop Johns, of the Episcopal Church. It was raining, and I did not attend.

Mrs. Greenhow, Mrs. Nelson's mother, and Tom William's Grandmother, died this morning at half after eight O'Clock.

I wrote to Cousin Clement Clay this morning, and then called to see Stevens a little while. Drizzling all day, and during the evening.

<u>Thursday, 23rd.</u> Mrs. Greenhow was buried this morning. I went to the church, and Anita went on to the cemetery.

<u>Anita: Thursday 23rd.</u> *I went Mrs. G.—Funeral, she was interred at Holy Wood. Mr. Burrows, the Baptist minister, preached a beautiful funeral sermon. When I reached home they told Mrs. Brewer was sick—her little daughter was born at six O'clock. I was the first person out of the room that heard her cry—*

<u>Friday, 24th.</u> Cold, sleet, rain and wind, all day and during the evening. The Yankees will have a hard time at Hatteras. We have heard that our troops in Eastern Kentucky, under Crittenden, sustained a defeat last Sunday: Genl. Zollicoffer is reported to have been killed, and it is said our loss in killed and wounded will amount to four hundred—the enemy's loss was also severe: five hundred our report says.

<u>Anita: Friday 24th.</u> *The weather is dreadful, hailing and raining all day long. I have not been out to exercise for an age.*

<u>Saturday 25th.</u> *I took my Music lesson I am learning the Whispering Winds.*

<u>Sunday 26th.</u> *We went to Church at eleven. Father Andrews preached a real good sermon on the love of the neighbor. In the evening we went to see Mrs. Williams and Nelson. Major and Mrs. Williams were there. I am feeling badly.*

Friday, 31st. We spent the evening at Mr. Maury's. Rained and sleeted at night.

My pay this month, Capt. Barksdale, was $158.00, and my Commutation, Capt. Whitfield, was $45.00.

February, 1862.

<u>Saturday, 1st.</u> Rainy all day. Nothing of especial interest transpiring.

<u>Anita: Saturday 1st of February.</u> It rained all day nearly. I took my Music lesson. Mrs. Stuart finished my collar for me.

<u>Sunday, 2nd.</u> Anita and I went to church in the morning, and took dinner at Mr. John Purcell's. Damp and raw at night.

<u>Anita: Sunday 2nd.</u> I went to Church at 11 O'clock, heard an excellent sermon, from there we went home with Mrs. John Purcell—and dined. We returned home about 4, layed down— After Tea we sat in the parlour.

<u>Monday, 3rd.</u> Snow fell last night and this morning. Rained pretty much all the afternoon and evening.

<u>Anita: Monday 3rd.</u> It snowed all morning. I sent for Dr. Dean to see me, he said I was getting along very well. In the morning I suffered with pain in my teeth—neuralgia, I suppose.

<u>Tuesday, 4th.</u> Cousin Edmund Withers, Lucy Duval and I, went to the African Church at night to hear Blind Tom play

the piano, sing, and speak: he has grown since I heard him in Washington last Winter, and has improved in his playing. He played "Fischer's Hornpipe" with his right hand, "Yankee Doodle" with his left, and sang "Dixie", all at the same time.

Anita: Tuesday 4th. I still suffer with the pain in my face. The Captain sent me some lager beer and nuts.

<u>Sunday, 9th.</u> Anita has been suffering with face ache and sick stomach for several days. The weather has been wet and disagreeable for a week past. We have a rumor to-day that Yankee vessels have run up to Florence, Alabama, on the Tennessee River. Rumors of foreign interference, fighting on Roanoke Island, &c. &c., are rife. Anita was taken with pain in the right side, short breathing and fever about nine P.M., which continued all night.

<u>Monday, 10th.</u> Anita had fever all night last night, but no nausea. I sent for Doctor Dean early in the morning: he said he would prefer waiting until the afternoon before doing anything. He returned at 3 P.M., and told me he thought my dear wife was threatened with pneumonia—he prescribed five grains of calomel to be given at once, and to be repeated at 10 P.M. Anita had no operation to-day. She had no nausea. I was at home nearly all day.

<u>Tuesday, 11th.</u> At one, A.M., Anita's right breast had five dry cups put on, and five wet ones were put on her back, or right shoulder and side. These gave her some relief from pain, but the fever continued unabated. She slept, however, from two until six, A.M. At seven, A.M., the five grain dose of Calomel

was repeated. At 11, A.M., Dr. Dean had a large blister put upon her right breast and back, and gave her the thirtieth of a grain of tarter emetic once every hour until three, P.M., at which time she had an operation on her bowels. She was very little nauseated. The fever abated after the medicine operated, and she had no more during the night. The blister drew well by six O'Clock, P.M., when it was removed, and a flax meal poultice substituted for it. She had signs of strangula during the night.

Wednesday, 12th. Anita slept from 11 last night until three this morning—then awoke for a little while, and slept at intervals until 8, A.M. Dr. Dean gave her no medicine during the day except a tea-spoonful of paregoric to allay griping pains in her bowels: he said she must be kept perfectly quiet. A good many of her friends called to-day, but were not allowed to see her. Mrs. Duval and Mrs. Stuart are the only ladies who wait on her—they, with Charlotte and myself, are her nurses. Fever again came on at noon to-day, and kept up all night. The weather is lovely to-day. Anita had some symptoms of miscarriage to-day. Doctor Dean candidly told me in the evening that my dear wife had a most trying complication of pleurisy and pneumonia, and a threating of miscarriage, in consequence of which her life was endangered. God alone knows how fervently I prayed to-night that this bitter affliction may be spared me. I have this night resolved to be, with God's help, a better man—and a Catholic. My wife's Christian, exemplary life, is a standing, burning rebuke upon me. Dr. Dean gave her two doses dover's powder, in pills, with three grains of calomel, at nine, P.M. after the blister was dressed. Anita talked a great deal all day, and wanderingly so at night, until she fell asleep at 11, P.M. She had no operation to-day.

Thursday, 13th. I talked to Anita freely about the Catholic Church to-day, and told her that I had last night determined to try and become a Catholic. Anita dozed at intervals until daylight. She seemed better about breakfast-time, and eat [sic] a cracker and drank a cup of tea. In a little while after this, about ten O'Clock, A.M., she had a miscarriage, and was feverish from that time until night. She has taken nothing but ice water and flaxseed tea since morning. I am with her almost constantly. Dr. Dean made an examination in the evening, and found that the miscarriage was apparently complete, without much hemorrhage. He directs that fifty drops of the elixir of opium should be given her at ten, and at midnight. Anita slept, but it was much interrupted, and she still seemed to be wandering in her mind. She had no operation.

Friday, 14th. Cloudy and damp. Anita took a cup of tea, and a couple of crackers, at breakfast, and said she felt better. Dr. Dean thinks her better, but says her tongue indicates some complication of her stomach. She dozed all the forenoon. I used on her a warm water anema [sic] at noon, and she had a very fair operation from her bowls. About three, P.M., she was taken with great shortness of breath, and complained of pain in her right side. Dr. Dean saw her about five, P.M., and told me she was worse—that he felt greatly encouraged in the morning, but that her condition then, (5 P.M.) was not so good, although he still believes she would get well after a tedious convalescence.

He said the shortness of breath and pain in the side looked as if a return of pleurisy was upon her, but that nothing could be done just then to alleviate it—the blister still being quite sore. The redness of the edges of her tongue, and her total indifference as to anything to eat looked as though her stomach was much disordered, and a dilation of her nostrils and tightness of skin on her nose and face showed she was far from being in a hopeful condition, and although Anita made herself out pretty well, she was, as he expressed it, miserably uncomfortable. He said she was disposed always to make herself out better than she really was, whereas patients most generally imagine themselves worse than they actually are.

He told me to give her milk toddy to compose her, and, failing in that, to give her the elixir of opium. The ladies dressed her blister by nine, P.M., and I gave her a milk toddy. She continued to breathe short, and with difficulty. She was extremely restless, getting no sleep atall scarcely, until midnight, when I gave her another milk toddy. I also gave her ice. I looked at her tongue, and found it still very bad. She complained of pain in her side and in her back, and really appeared to be suffering more than she could bear for any great length of time.

Saturday, 15th. About half after one, A.M., poor Anita seemed to have been overcome with want of sleep and with pain, and told me that she believed she had been sinking for the past three days and must soon succumb to the disease. I was almost frantic, and was going to go up stairs for Dr. Brewer, who is an Army Assistant Surgeon, and who is staying at Mrs. Duval's: he attended our dear Angel baby in his last illness.

Anita appeared to be entirely collected, told me not to weep and make her worse, but to go and first ask Mrs. Duval to come in. Mrs. Duval came in, and, after some consideration, said she thought there must be some unusual nervous excitement, and said I had better try a dose of the elixir of opium. This composed Anita entirely. She ceased coughing and fell into a profound sleep about two, A.M., which she enjoyed until 8, A.M., when she awoke, and said she was much better. She asked for a cup of tea and a cracker, and enjoyed both. She fell asleep again, and waked up about eleven, when she asked for a little sangaree. I gave her some lemonade, and ice. Dr. Dean came about one, P.M., and said she was very much better indeed: so much so that he would not return to see her to-day unless sent for. He said she required no medicine: that her fever was gone.

Anita slept most of the afternoon—evidently the effects of the opium she took last night. I went to the Office from six to eight, P.M. The weather was abominable all day, raining, sleeting and snowing, in succession. Anita had no operation on her bowels to-day. She took a cup of tea at eight, P.M. Her breathing was a little short at night, but I gave her no opium—she was restless, and complained that I went to sleep, leaving her awake. She said she laid for a long time in a sort of trance, after midnight, and wanted me to help her, but could not get me to do so. I gave her a little milk toddy twice during the night. She had a very good pulse, but seemed to be very weak. Mrs. Stuart was not well this morning, and Mrs. Wootten dressed Anita's hair. Anita coughs very little, but that little troubles her a great deal.

Sunday, 16th. Beautiful day overhead—snow melting. I remained at home the entire day. Anita has had no fever all day: no operation on her bowels. She passes a little blood every day. She complains of being extremely weak; but her pulse is good, and we do not think she is more feeble than ought to be anticipated. She is disposed to complain of us all. Mrs. Stuart continued to be unwell, and Mrs. Wootten again combed Anita's hair this morning. Anita took a cup of tea and a cracker at breakfast, and some buttermilk which Aaron, (who is a clerk in our office), procured for her, a little later in the day. She took some chicken broth twice in the course of the afternoon. She took no medicine during the day. She slept from about two, P.M., to a little after three, P.M., and from four until six, P.M. She does not talk in her sleep anymore, but is a little fanciful in her notions when she first wakes from her naps. Dr. Dean sent us word at nightfall that he was sick and could not come to see Anita to-day. We dressed her blister and she went to sleep at nine O'Clock, P.M. She took a little chicken broth for supper, and appeared to be much better. She slept well all night, waking once or twice.

Monday, 17th. Dr. Dean was too unwell to call to-day. I wrote him a note as to Anita's condition, and he replied that there was no necessity for having any other physician to see her: should such necessity arise, he would ask his friend Dr. Cunningham to call around. I spent most of the morning at the Office. Miserable weather. Trees covered with sleet. Raining and sloppy. Anita slept a good part of the forenoon, after they changed her sheets, and fixed the bed. She has no fever. She had a natural operation on her bowls about eleven, A.M. She slept nearly all the afternoon. She took a little milk and water, with a cracker, for her tea, and a glass of lemonade later in the evening. I went to the Office from 6 to 8, P.M. Anita slept well during the night.

Tuesday, 18th. I wrote to Mrs. Dwyer to-day, finishing Anita's letter of the 9th. Anita has been improving all day. No fever. I gave her an anema after breakfast, and she had a very good operation on her bowels. I attended to my Official duties to-day. Some of Anita's lady friends sat with her during the morning. Anita took a soft-boiled egg for breakfast—she took a little beef tea, a little rice, and a little buttermilk at intervals during the day.

Both houses of Congress met to-day—Mr. Bocock, of Va., elected Speaker without opposition. Rain at night. Cousin Clement and Cousin Jeannie arrived here in the afternoon, and took a room at Mrs. Duval's. Cousin Jeannie sat with Anita in the evening. Dressed her blister at night.

Anita: Sunday 9th-18th. February. I was taken sick, had high fever all night, and continued to have it for a week. I had a terrible attack of pneumonia and a miscarriage. I layed dangerously ill for several days. Dr. Dean felt very uneasy about me. My dear Husband nursed me tenderly through my sickness. One evening we talked about Religion, he promised me seriously he would try and become a member of the Catholic Church. Mrs. Duval and Mrs. Stuart were extremely kind to me. They used to dress my blisters and poultices. Mrs. Wootten, another kind friend, arranged my hair for me every morning for a week. All my other friends outside were exceedingly kind to me also in coming to see me, and sending me **nice** things to tempt my appetite.

Cousin Jeannie and Clement arrived here on the evening of the 18th.
of Feb. The day the permanent Congress met. I was still confined to
my bed when they came. Cousin Lawson was also in the city for a
few days, on his way to Knoxville, Tenn.

<u>*Wednesday, 19th.*</u> Rained steadily all day. Weather quite mild. I
was at the Office as usual, coming home a little while at noon
to see how my wife was getting on. Cousin Jeannie spent most
of the day with Anita. I was tendered the appointment of
temporary Major in the Adjutant General's Department yesterday, and declined it to-day. Cousin Edmund Withers called
in the afternoon. I think Anita has heard too much talking to-
day—from this, or from some other cause, she seems to be a
little feverish to-night. This passed off after her company dis-
persed. She has had no operation on her bowels to-day.
Cousin Clement's health is much better, apparently, than it
has been for some time. Cousin Jeannie is fatter than I have
ever seen her.

<u>*Thursday, 20th.*</u> Pleasant day. A good many ladies, at least a
dozen, called to see Anita to-day—Mrs. Col. Chilton sat all the
morning, and until two, P.M., with her. Cousin Jeannie has
had a great many calls to-day: —She and Cousin Edmund
Withers went to hear blind Tom play the piano in the evening.
Anita had three operations on her bowels to-day—she has no
fever. Her upper lip is somewhat swollen, and gives her some
pain. I sent for Dr. Dean, after tea, fearing she might be in-
clined to Erysipelas: he promised to come, but did not do so.
We put a little laudanum and water on a rag, and laid it on
her lip—she went to sleep about ten, P.M.

Friday, 21st. Fine day. Dr. Dean came to see Anita in the morning, and said her lip was swollen from a gum boil. He told her that the whole of the after birth had not yet passed off, and hence the offensiveness of her courses for the past two or three days. He told her to use an injection of warm water for the womb, which she did. She had an operation from her bowels to-day. She slept very little to-day, on account of the number of visitors she had. Mrs. Toombs called to say farewell to her—Mrs. Toombs is just breaking up housekeeping, to go to Georgia. Mrs. Dr. Trent sent my wife some sweet flowers, and some delicious wafers to-day. Mrs. Duval and Mrs. Stuart dressed her blister in the evening—it has nearly healed up. Cousin Clement went to hear blind Tom play in the evening. Cousin Jeannie, of course, had a room full of company all day.

The Rev. G.V. Macdona, who came to Texas from Ireland about four years since, (he was then a mere youth), who became a minister in the Presbyterian Church, and who has since become a Clergyman in the Episcopal Church, called to see us to-day. He has a Parish in Virginia, but wants to return to Ireland.

Saturday, 22nd. To-day is my thirty fifth birthday. Rained steadily all day, and during the evening. Dr. Dean came to see Anita in the morning—he removed the small portion of the after birth which had not been thrown off, and he lanced a gum bile [sic] on Anita's upper lip. He says she is getting on finely, and will improve ever more rapidly than heretofore, now that the two sources of irritation above mentioned have been removed. Genl. Cooper, Col. Myers, Col. Chilton and I went up to the Capitol at noon to witness the inauguration of President Davis: the crowd was so great that Genl. Cooper and I left. Everything passed off as pleasantly as possible, considering the rain poured down during all the ceremonies. In the evening Anita was much better: so much so that I went to the reception at the President's. Capt. and Mrs. Myers, from North Carolina, came up from the Exchange, and took Cousin Clement, Cousin Jeannie and myself with them. Cousin Jeannie, I think, was more handsomely dressed, and the most stylish looking lady in the house. The reception was fully attended, and the company was very fair. Cousin Jeannie and Mrs. Myers came in to see Anita before they went to the President's—the ladies in our house come in to see their dresses.

Sunday, 23rd. Cloudy to-day, but no rain. I was at home nearly all day, and during the whole evening. Anita is improving steadily: she sat up on the sofa for two or three hours to-day. She had to use an anema. Several ladies have been with her during the day and evening. Mrs. Myers came in after tea. Cousin Clement spent the afternoon and evening at the President's. The temperature is quite mild to-day.

Monday, 24th. I was busy at the Office to-day. Anita was up when I returned home at three, P.M. She is much better to-day. No action on her bowels. The wind was unusually high all day. Clear and mild—a little cool in the afternoon and evening.

Thursday, 25th. Very fine day. Cousin Lawson arrived here in the afternoon. Anita has been improving all day. She used an anema to-day. I got her a couple of partridges: the Doctor called to see her, and said she could eat a little of almost anything that she desired. Several ladies called to see her during the day. She sat up, and walked about the room a good deal. She is still very weak. The Dr. says all the after birth has passed off.

Wednesday, 26th. Pleasant in the forenoon. Begun to rain about two, P.M., and continued all the afternoon and evening. Anita sat up pretty much all day. Her lady friends are sending her many nice little things to eat. She is steadily convalescing.

Thursday, 27th. Beautiful day. Anita is still improving.

Friday, 28th. Fine day. Day of Fasting and Prayer. I went up to attend service at the Catholic Church at the usual Sunday hour, eleven O'Clock, but found that Services had just closed, having begun at ten, A.M. I went up to Mr. John Purcell's and remained an hour or so. Anita is getting on very well. Churches all very much crowded to-day.

My pay this month, Capt. Barksdale, was $158.00, and my commutation, Capt. Whitfield, was $45.00.

March, 1862.

<u>Saturday, 1st.</u> President Davis has to-day proclaimed Martial law over Richmond, and the county adjacent for ten miles in all directions. Cold and raw all day. Anita complained of sick head-ache in the afternoon, and went to bed early. Cousin Clement has been coughing a good deal this afternoon, and at night.

<u>Anita: Saturday, March 1st.</u> *I walked into the parlour this morning for the first time in several weeks.*

<u>Sunday, 2nd.</u> John Minor Botts was arrested this morning, on a charge of disaffection to the Government—many other less important arrests have been made during the day. I went to the Catholic Church in the morning. Anita is improving. She put on her hoops and corset, and dressed up nicely to-day. Damp and raw all day.

<u>Anita: Sunday, 2nd.</u> *I went up to Cousin Jeannie's room.*

<u>3rd.</u> *I went up there again, played a little on the piano.*

Monday, 3rd. Wet and cold to-day. Very windy at night, and alternately raining and clear. Two or three fires at night. Anita is getting better.

Tuesday, 4th. Clear and windy all day—not very cold. I was occupied at the Office all day. Anita is still improving.

Anita: Tuesday, March 4th. I had a good deal of company today, a fine bright day it is. My dear brother is twenty one years old today. We received a sweet letter from him, and also the proclamation he translated to the people of New Mexico.

Wednesday, 5th. Pleasant day. I took Anita out riding in a close carriage about noon: —She is improving steadily. Bishop Wilmer (for Alabama) was consecrated at St. Paul's to-day.

Thursday, 6th. I took Anita to Mr. John Purcell's about noon, and left her there for the day. Got quite cold in the afternoon, and snowed all the evening. We took dinner at Mr. Purcell's and got home before dark. I went to Dr. Conway's at ten in the evening, and remained until midnight. It was an entertainment in compliment to the graduating class at the Medical College. I met many acquaintances, had a delicious supper, plenty of wines, &c., and spent a most agreeable evening generally.

Friday, 7th. Clear and cool all day. Anita did not go out to-day. Cousin Jeannie and I called to see Mrs. Myers at the Exchange after tea. Beautiful moonlight night.

<u>*Saturday, 8th.*</u> Fine day. Anita rode out with Cousin Jeannie during the day—she had headache at night.

<u>*Sunday, 9th.*</u> Anita and I went to church in the morning—we rode going, and walked returning. Anita had head-ache and tooth ache all the afternoon. We heard to-day that our iron clad vessel at Norfolk, the Virginia, had sunk the Frigate Cumberland, destroyed the Frigate Congress, badly used up the Steam Frigate Minnesota, and destroyed two gun boats.

<u>*Anita: Sunday 9th.*</u> *My Husband and myself went to Church at eleven, I for the first time in a month. Father Mac preached.*

<u>*Monday, 10th.*</u> All Richmond was elated to-day with the brilliant achievements of the Virginia. Anita had a jaw tooth pulled out to-day. Fine weather.

<u>*Tuesday, 11th.*</u> I was quite unwell all day. I took ten grains of blue mass last night. I took two anti-bilious pills to-night.

<u>*Anita: Tuesday 11th.*</u> *I took a little walk today. Bishop McGill came to see us, also Mrs. and Miss Cowardice, Mrs. Nelson and Miss Greenhow.*

Wednesday I took a music lesson. Mr. Edmundson came around to see us yesterday evening. I walked as far as the Office.

<u>*Wednesday, 12th.*</u> I was quite feeble all day, and had head-ache. I was at the Office all day, however.

Thursday, 13th. I was better to-day. Anita and I took dinner at Dr. Wayt's—Mr. and Mrs. Wootten were also invited, and some young ladies were present. Rained a little in the afternoon.

Friday, 14th. I was busy at the Office all day. Cloudy and damp. Rumors of a victory of Confederates, under Van Dorn, over the Federals, under Curtis, were rife on the streets to-day.

Saturday, 15th. Rained hard to-day. Cloudy and damp at night. Some of us went from Mrs. Duval's (Cousin Clement and Cousin Jeannie, Mr. and Mrs. Wootten, and little Lucy Duval with myself) to hear Harry McGarthy in his comic songs, and recitations and to see his jigs. He is decidedly a genius.

Sunday, 16th. Anita and I went to church in the morning. The ceremonies were very imposing. The exposition of the Holy Sacrament was made—the beginning of a forty hours devotion—and a procession marched round the inside of the church. The Bishop, (Rev. Father McGill), all the Priests, Sisters, Scholars and orphans, assisted. Anita and I took dinner at Mr. John Purcell's. Fine weather.

Monday, 17th. Fine weather still. Cousin Jeannie, Anita and I, went up to call at Tom William's. Mrs. J.G. Walker is at Mrs. Williams', and has a little daughter three days old.

Tuesday, 18th. The Cabinet of the Permanent Government was organized to-day by the confirmation by the Senate of the following gentlemen: [sic]

Anita: Tuesday, 18th. *Feast of the Arch-Angel Gabrielle. I went to Holy Communion this morning—so did many of my friends. In the afternoon I took a very long walk with Cousin Jeannie.*

Wednesday, 19th. Anita and I took dinner at Mrs. Nelson's to-day—pleasant weather.

Thursday, 20th. Rained at intervals during the day.

Friday, 21st. Showery to-day—weather quite mild. The President went up to Gordonsville to-day, and of course the City is all agog as to the object of his visit. It may be that he believes a great battle is soon to be fought by the Army of the Potomac.

Saturday, 22nd. Mild and cloudy. I was busy at the Office during the day. I dined with Mr. Cranz to-day. Brig. Genl. H.A. Wise, his son-in-law Mr. [sic] and his son-in-law's brother, Mr. [sic], Captain Webb, of the "Teazer," Mr. John Purcell, Judge Lyons, Dr. Peachy, Captain [sic] , of the "Governor's Guard," 4th. Regt. Va. Cavalry, Major Staunard, an Aid-de-Camp of Genl. Wise, myself and Mr. [sic] , composed the party. One or two of the above happened in while we were at dinner. We sat down about 5, P.M., and left about 9, P.M. We passed a most agreeable time. Genl. Wise did good service with his tongue: Dr. Peachy is also a most agreeable dinner companion. The dinner was a very nice one, and the wines were delicious.

Anita: Saturday, 22nd. *My Angel boy would have been 2 years old today. I took a Music lesson—remained at home all day.*

Sunday, 23rd. Anita and I went to church in the morning—fine weather.

Anita: Sunday, 23rd. I feel pretty well. The Capt. and myself went to Church at 11 O'clock.

Monday, 24th. The new Secretary of War, Mr. Geo. W. Randolph, took charge of his office to-day. Anita and I rode out to see Miss Picot in the afternoon, but she was not at home; we afterwards went to see Mrs. Walker, at Tom Williams'. Genl. Walker arrived here from Fredericksburg with his brigade in the evening, en route to North Carolina.

Tuesday, 25th. Washington and his family reached here from South Carolina to-day. Wilcox arrived here from Manassas with his Alabama brigade to-day: Col. Sydenham Moore, of the 12th Ala., and Lt. Col. O'Neal of the 9th Ala. Regt., called to see Cousin Clement and Cousin Jeannie, my wife and I, in the evening. Cousin Thomas Adams was also here. Pleasant weather—rather frosty at night.

Wednesday, 26th. Fine day. Washington and his wife spent the evening with us.

Thursday, 27th. Anita and Cousin Jeannie went out visiting to-day—they, and Cousin Clement, with Mrs. Wootten, went to Metropolitan Hall in the evening, to witness some "War Illustrations."

Friday, 28th. Beautiful day—nothing special going on.

Anita: Saturday, 29th. I determined to visit Salisbury—I took my last Music lesson.

<u>Saturday, 29th.</u> Anita has determined to make Mrs. Myers a visit in Salisbury, N.C. Damp day.

<u>Sunday, 30th.</u> Damp and drizzly. Anita and I took a carriage and went to Church in the morning—were then called to see Mrs. Walker at Tom Williams'. Remained at home in the afternoon and evening. Anita is ready to be off to-morrow afternoon—she expects to stay in Petersburg to-morrow night.

<u>Monday, 31st.</u> I left the Office at half after one, P.M., so as to help my dear wife get ready for her trip. Anita took a carriage in the morning, and called to say adieu to several of her lady friends: she got her dinner, and I took her to the depot in time to be off in the 3 O'Clock train for Petersburg, where she is to rest for the night. Mrs. Winder, with her daughter and son were my wife's traveling companions. Anita took Charlotte and six trunks. I have a very bad cold in my head, and felt badly all day. Cousin Jeannie insisted on my going with cousin Clement, Dr. Read and herself to see Mrs. Davis in the evening. Mrs. Davis was looking as well as I ever saw her, talked a great deal, and made herself unusually sociable. We met Mr. Orr, of S.C., Mr. Yancey, of Ala., Gov. Letcher, of Va., and the President himself. Both Mrs. Davis and the President were very particular in their inquiries after my wife, and spoke most kindly of her, as they always do. We returned home about nine, having made a visit of about an hour.

<u>*Anita: Monday, 31st.*</u> *I made a good many calls, in the evening about 2 O'clock I started for Salisbury in company with Mrs. Gen. Winder. I reached Salisbury at 3 O'clock A. M. Captain Winder of the Navy took care of me after I parted with Mrs. W. Capt. and Mrs. Myers were up all night long waiting for me.*

My pay this month, Capt. Barksdale, was $158.00, and my commutation, Capt. Whitfield, was $45.00.

April, 1862.

<u>Tuesday, 1st.</u> I felt badly all day—head-ache and heavy discharge from my nose. I took tea at Dr. Wayts', after writing a short letter to Anita.

<u>Wednesday, 2nd.</u> Got a telegram from Edmondston at Raleigh, saying Anita passed through that City yesterday. I wrote to Anita in the evening, and then went up to see Mrs. Nelson. Had a very bad night—suffered pain in my left nostril which kept me awake from two, P.M., pretty much until morning. Mr. and Mrs. Wootten left us this morning.

<u>Thursday, 3rd.</u> I suffered a great deal of pain in my head to-day: considerable discharge from my nose. Called to see Mrs. Washington in the afternoon. Remained at home in the evening. This has been really a lovely day out of doors. Mrs. Stuart left us this morning, to join her husband at Gordonsville. Col. Blanton Duncan, Lt. Col. Scott, 4th Ala., (formerly member of Congress from California) Mr. S. S. Scott, of Ala., and Mrs. Philip Clayton spent the evening with Cousin Jeannie. Mr. Gwin arrived here from Baltimore to-day. I wrote Capt. Myers a note to-night.

Anita: Thursday, 3rd. Several called on me today. We took a walk in the morning, I weighed only a hundred and four. Salisbury is a very quiet place, such like the country. I wrote to my old man today.

Friday, 4th. I suffered greatly from my cold to-day. No war news of interest.

Anita: Friday, 4th. I coughed a great deal last night. I [felt] rather badly this morn—

Saturday, 5th. Disappointed in not getting a letter from my dear wife. I moved my room at the Office to-day—instead of having seven gentlemen writing in the same room with me, I now have only one.

Sunday, 6th. My cold is a little better to-day. I went to church and heard Bishop McGill preach. Beautiful day. A large number of troops from Genl. Joe Johnston's Army are passing through the city to-day, en route to Yorktown, where a great fight is expected soon to occur. I took tea at Mr. James Purcell's, and spent the evening there. I got two letters from my dear wife to-day—one dated the 3rd, which came by mail, and one dated the 5th., brought me by Mr. Myer Myers, a brother of Captain Myers. I was truly rejoiced to hear from my beloved Anita.

Monday, 7th. Richmond is elate to-day with the news that a great battle between ours and the Yankee troops was fought at Pittsburg on the Tennessee River, on the 6th., in which we were completely victorious. We lost our gallant Commander in chief, Albert Sidney Johnston, which has cast a gloom over the great victory. Bad, rainy day. Troops still passing through to Yorktown—Nothing new from there.

<u>*Tuesday, 8th.*</u> Rained slowly all day, and at night. No additional news of interest. I took dinner at Mrs. Nelson's. No letter from Anita to-day: I wrote to her last night, and sent her a letter from Joe and some papers. I remained at home all the evening.

<u>*Wednesday, 9th.*</u> Rained all day. I wrote to Anita in the afternoon. We received news to-day that Buell re-enforced Grant's beaten army on the night of the 6th., attacked Beauregard on the 7th., fought until 1, P.M., and re-captured a good deal of property of various kinds which we took from them on the 6th. Beauregard retired to Corinth, and is being re-enforced by Van Dorn's Army from Arkansas, a number of Regiments from Chattanooga, Tennessee, and all the forces he can assemble from Alabama, Mississippi and Louisiana. It seems as though a great fight must soon be fought at Corinth, before which all the rest must sink into comparative insignificance. Meantime large numbers of troops continue to pass through here from Joe Johnston's Army, en route to Yorktown, where another conflict of arms seems imminent.

<u>*Thursday, 10th.*</u> Rainy, disagreeable day. Nothing special going on.

<u>*Friday, 11th.*</u> Fine day. Cousin Jeannie left early this morning to make a visit to Mr. Lay's sister, (Mrs. Watkins), who lives about 30 or 40 miles from Richmond. We received news to-day that Huntsville, Alabama, has been occupied by the

Yankees. Cousin Clement was right sick in the afternoon—he took a little chloroform, which nauseated him, and caused him to throw up his dinner. In the evening he was better. Stevens and Wm. E. Jones, of my class, spent the evening with us. I heard from my dear wife to-day—she is improving in health. Genl. J.E. Johnston and staff are in the City.

Saturday, 12th. It is reported that Fort Pulaski, near Savannah, Georgia, has surrendered to the Federals, after a bombardment of two days and nights—the surrender is reported to have taken place the day before yesterday. Genl. G.W. Smith and staff are in the City: Genl. S. called at the Office this evening. Beautiful day. Washington, Jones, Wm. E., and I, went up and took tea with Tom Williams at his mother's this evening.

Sunday, 13th. I went to church in the morning. The services were long, being Palm Sunday, and the Bishop's sermon was short. I took dinner at Mr. James Purcell's, after calling to see Mrs. Genl. Rodes at Mr. Charles Purcell's. Toombs' Brigade passed down main street late in the afternoon, en route to Yorktown. Toombs made himself very conspicuous, and was evidently "intipsicated with regard to." He would lead one regiment by a given point, and then charge back to head a succeeding regiment—bowing to the ladies, and even taking his hat clear off, in recognition of their handkerchief waving, &c. In the evening I walked up to the Spotswood Hotel for a while. Dr. Brewer's brother, a Lieutenant in the "Washington Artillery," La. Volunteers, got here this afternoon, and sleeps in my room to-night. Fine weather.

Monday, 14th. Genl. Lee, G.W. Smith, J.E. Johnston, and the President had a long consultation to-day, and I expect a fight on the peninsula will take place to-morrow or the day after. I got letters from my wife's Aunt in Dublin to-day—they were dated January 23rd., '62. I wrote to Anita to-night. Mild day, but somewhat cloudy. Washington took tea with me, and spent the evening. Cousin Jeannie returned this afternoon from her visit to the country.

Tuesday, 15th. Pleasant day. I was busy at the Office as usual. I called at Mr. Maury's in the evening. Tom Williams came down to see Cousin Clement and Jeannie, and spent an hour or so in the evening.

Wednesday, 16th. Genl. Longstreet's Division of the Army of the Potomac passed through the City to-day, en route to York-town. There were some ten thousand men, Infantry, Artillery, and Cavalry. Brig. Genl. A.P. Hill led off the Infantry—Brig. Genl. Pendleton the Artillery, and Brig. Genl. Stuart the Cavalry. Jones, Wm. E, and Beverly Robertson were with their Cavalry Regiments. The Infantry passed down Main Street—the Cavalry down Franklin, and the Artillery down Franklin, to the square, and thence down Main. It was a grand sight.

I heard from my dear wife to-day, and am truly grateful to learn that she is improving in health: I write almost every day. Beautiful, spring like day. The French Minister, Count Merciér, arrived here from Washington this evening: of course innumerable conjectures are indulged as to what his object is in coming here just now.

Thursday, 17th. Lovely day—Mild as Spring sure enough. Nothing special going on.

Friday, 18th. This has been a stirring day in Richmond. It seems to have transpired that the French Minister has come here from Washington, on a mere tour of observation—that the Lincoln Government have affected the tone of conquerors already, and assured him that the rebellion would be crushed out in three months, at the farthest. We have it reported that the Federals have attacked Forts Jackson and St. Philip, on the Mississippi, below New Orleans, with their Mortar Fleet. There has been some farther demonstration upon Savannah, Georgia, and a reported attack upon Fort Mason, Georgia. It is said, too, that Fredericksburg, Va., is in the hands of the Federals—that 15,000, under McDowell, are there. There are reports, also, of an expected move against Stone Wall Jackson, and of his having fallen back. We have nothing from the Peninsula, to-day, although the street rumor is that there has been more fighting there. Very mild all day. Sprinkled rain a little about tea time.

Saturday, 19th. Drizzling rain during the day. No Military news of importance.

Sunday, 20th. Rained a good deal to-day. No Military news of consequence—none atall, in fact. I went to church in the morning. This being Easter Sunday, the ceremonies at the church were very elaborate, the Bishop (McGill) saying Mass. The music was very fine. Mr. Dacoeniel's new Mass was played. I took dinner at Mr. Jno. Purcell's and wrote to my wife in the afternoon. Remained at home in the evening.

<u>*Monday, 21st.*</u> Rainy, disagreeable day. Cousin Clement dined with Monsieur Merciér, the French Minister, at Mr. James Lyon's country seat: besides the host and hostess, and the two gentlemen above named, the party consisted of the Secretary of Legation, of Hon. Mr. Gwin, Mr. W.M. Browne, Mr. Perkins, of La. Mr. Wyndham Robinson, Senator Conrad of La., Monsieur Paul, the resident French Consul, and some one else whom I do not now recall (Judge Meredith). It was a most agreeable entertainment. Washington took dinner with me. I took tea at Tom William's mother. No military news of special importance.

<u>*Tuesday, 22nd.*</u> It is said that the French Minister left for Washington to-day. Fine weather. Washington has been ordered to Texas, and I have been struggling with myself, all the afternoon and evening, to get my own consent to Anita's going with him home. I think the trip would benefit her, and yet I am so selfish as to wish she may not prefer to go. It is very hard for me to think, even, of being so far from my dear wife. Miss Dean, daughter of Dr. Dean, was married at the Monumental Church, this evening, to Dr. Lyons, son of Mr. James Lyons, and all of this City. Cousin Jeannie, Mrs. Duval and Mrs. Abbott attended. It was a grand affair.

<u>*Wednesday, 23rd.*</u> Busy at the Office until two, P.M. Went over to Petersburg in the afternoon.

<u>*Thursday, 24th.*</u> Traveled all day, and got to Salisbury, N.C., at half after two O'Clock at night. Went to Capt. Myers', and found my dear wife much improved in health, but still nothing like so strong as I had trusted she would be.

<u>*Anita:*</u> *The Captain came to see me the morning of the 25th. April, he spent six days in Salisbury very pleasantly. The weather I am sorry to say was disagreeable, raining nearly all the time.*

<u>Wednesday, 30th.</u> Rained pretty much all day. I spent most of the day at Capt. Myers'. I am having a most charming visit.

My pay, Capt. Barksdale, was $158.00, and my Commutation, Capt. Whitfield, was $48.00, during this month.

May, 1862.

<u>Thursday, 1st.</u> I left Salisbury on my return to Richmond about ten O'Clock at night.

<u>Anita: May 1st.</u> Thursday, the Captain left for Richmond this evening. I don't believe I can go to Texas if New Orleans is surrendered.

The Capt. telegraphed to me on Sunday, June 1st. to go to Rich— by first opportunity. My friends advise me not to leave until we hear of the result of the battle. I feel very anxious about my Husband. Capt. Myers is also in Richmond.

<u>Friday, 2nd.</u> Missed the connection at Raleigh, and laid over all day. Saw Edmondston, and staid [sic] at his room. Saw Mrs. Brewer. Took a ride with Genl. Martin in the afternoon out to the military encampment. Took tea at Genl. Martin's. Raleigh is a beautiful place. Fine day.

<u>Saturday, 3rd.</u> Was detained a while in Petersburg. Saw Cousins Clement and Jeannie. Came over in same train with Mr. Mallory, Sec. of Navy, and Mr. Randolph, Sec. War, both of whom were returning from Norfolk to Richmond. I reached Richmond about half after nine O'Clock, P.M.

Sunday, 4th. Gentlemen at the office all glad to see me. I went to church in the morning, and heard Bishop McGill. Took dinner at Mr. James Purcell's, and tea at Mr. Jno. Purcell's.

Monday, 5th. Worked hard in the office to-day. Took dinner at Genl. Cooper's. I am going to take a room at Genl. Cooper's house, although I am sorry enough for having ever determined to do so. I am infinitely better off at Mrs. Duval's. Rained all day.

Tuesday, 6th. Pleasant day. Moved up to Genl. Cooper's. Spent the evening at Mrs. Duval's—Cousin Clement was there.

Wednesday, 7th. Confused reports of a fight below Williamsburg on Monday last: Richmond greatly excited.

Thursday, 8th. It seems that Longstreet's Division of the Army of the Peninsula, the rear guard of the Army, had a brilliant fight with a portion of McClellan's forces on Monday last, in which we repulsed the Yankees, and took upwards of three hundred prisoners: heavy loss on both sides. It further appears that Whiting's brigade, or rather his division, had an affair with the enemy near Barhamsville, in New Kent County yesterday, and drove his forces to their gun boats.

Friday, 9th. Fine weather. Richmond is wild with all sorts of rumors to-day. Upwards of three hundred Yankee prisoners, taken near Williamsburg, arrived here last night. I saw the breast plates which were taken yesterday from a Yankee Officer who was sent down from some part of Western Virginia where he was captured. They are made of iron, and cover the chest completely. We hear that Jackson fought and whipped the Yankees near Staunton on yesterday.

Saturday, 10th. Norfolk was evacuated to-day, I believe.

Sunday, 11th. I was kept at the office until after church time to-day. I took dinner at Capt. Maynard's.

Monday, 12th. It is stated that the Merrimack-Virginia, *our Navy*, was blown up on yesterday morning: This news has created the most profound sensation of all the events of the war.

Wednesday, 14th. Great excitement in the city to-day, caused by the appearance of the Yankee iron-clad steamers Monitor and Galena, and some wooden gun-boats near the obstructions on the James River about eight miles below this point. We were very near sending off valuable books and papers to Columbia, S.C. The vessels threw only a few shells at our battery.

Thursday, 15th. Matters quieted down to-day. The Governor, Common Council and President have announced their determination to defend Richmond to the last extremity. The enemy's vessels shelled our batteries from 7, A.M., until about noon, when they retired. We lost five men killed and a few wounded—Midshipman named Carroll was one of the killed. Great excitement amongst all classes of the population.

Friday, 16th. I went to Mass at Nine O'Clock, A.M. Bishop McGill gave a short and very pretty lecture, in the course of which he counseled all who were able to do so, and who were of no service here, to leave the City; whilst all who could be of use were to remain and defend their homes with their lives. He was truly patriotic and Christian in his advice. I wrote to my dear wife after services were over. All is reported quiet at the batteries this morning.

Sunday, 18th. I attended church this morning, and heard a beautiful sermon from Bishop McGill upon the teachings of the Catholic Church touching the classes of persons outside the pale of the Church, so to speak, who would not be eternally lost. The sermon was as good as any I have ever heard — the clearest, I think, I ever listened to.

Sunday, 25th. I went to church in the morning, dined at Mr. James Purcell's and walked out to Mr. Cowardin's in the afternoon. During the past week the Yankees have gotten up within five miles of Richmond, and a good deal of skirmishing has taken place. We can hear the cannonading in the City. We have had two or three days of wet weather the past week.

Tuesday, 27th. Beautiful day, although it promised rain early in the morning. Captain Maynard and I rode out, in the afternoon, to within sight of Mechanicsburg, where we saw Yankee pickets, and a Yankee flag. We heard heavy cannonading, and volley after volley of musketry out towards Hanover Court House: a heavy skirmish, if not quite a battle has evidently taken place not more than eight or ten miles from Richmond to-day. I met General Lee going out with some of his staff, trying to learn what was the amount of the fight. The Yankees had up two balloons all the afternoon — the balloons appeared to be eight or ten miles distant from each other, and probably the same distance from Richmond.

<u>Wednesday, 28th.</u> Captain Maynard and I rode down to Drewry's Bluff, about eight miles below the City, in the afternoon, and examined our batteries there. The place really seems impregnable against any river attack, and can only be taken by land approaches. We saw Capts. Lee, Tucker, Chetard, and other Naval Officers who are in charge of the river obstructions, and of the land batteries. We got back to the City after dark a while. Nothing special on our lines around the City to-day.

<u>Thursday, 29th.</u> Groner went up the canal a few miles with our Office papers to-day. Nothing of importance has transpired on our lines to-day. Fine weather.

<u>Friday, 30th.</u> Pleasant in forenoon, but terrific thunder storm, with wind and rain, all the afternoon and evening. No matter of moment transpired on our lines to-day, so far as heard from. The storm was terrific at night.

<u>Saturday, 31st.</u> A portion of our forces attacked the Yankee command which is this side of the Chickahominy, to-day, about six miles below the City. Genl. Longstreet's and Genl. Whiting's Divisions were engaged, and drove the enemy from his redoubts, riflepits, and camp, with what loss of life or wounded on his side we cannot tell. Our loss in killed and wounded was very severe. Genl. J.E. Johnston was wounded in the shoulder just before night, and had to give up the

command. Genl. Rodes was wounded, and great numbers of others high in rank.

Anita: May 31st. Salisbury. *The battle near Richmond commenced today—as far as we have heard they have continued fighting for three days.*

My pay, Capt. Barksdale, was $158.00, and my Commutation, Capt. Whitfield, was $33.75.

June, 1862.

Sunday, 1st. Very warm to-day, this the first of Summer. I went to church in the morning. General Lee has been put in immediate command of the Army in Virginia, on account of the wound Genl. Johnston received yesterday being of so serious a character as to force him to keep in the house for some time. I went to the Spotswood Hotel at two O'Clock, P.M., and saw Dr. Peachey amputate the right arm of Surgeon Gallard, of Genl. G.W. Smith's Division: the arm was fractured just above the elbow joint, by a minnié ball, in the fight yesterday. Dr. Petticolas and Dr. Brewer, with Dr. Scott and Surgeon General Moore assisted. Several other physicians were present. Dr. Peachey gave his patient chloroform, and amputated the arm beautifully.

Richmond was full of the wildest rumors all day, most of which proved to be utterly false. There was a little fighting early in the morning, but the lines were quiet the rest of the day. Col. Gorgas and I walked down main street in the afternoon, and found it crowded with people. We must have met two or three hundred stragglers from the Army—most of them with their arms. There seems to be a melancholy want of system and discipline in our whole Army affairs: Citizens going to camp, and soldiers coming in without let or hindrance.

Anita: June 2nd. *I have written to the Capt. and sent the letter by persons going. Mrs. Myers and myself went to the depot this evening to hear the news. They have stopped fighting to bury their dead.*

Friday, 6th. Nothing of special importance has occurred on our lines the past five days. We have had unusually heavy rains, and all the streams are very high.

Anita: Saturday, June 7th. *I left Salisbury, Mr. Burke was my escort.*

Sunday, 8th. Anita reached here from Salisbury this afternoon: she was right unwell with sick headache. To-day has been a fine day. A little skirmishing on part of the lines. I feel happy, now, to get my dear wife back with me again. We have our old room at Mrs. Duval's—the front room, on the third floor, which we occupied when we first came to Richmond a year ago, and in which our dear baby sickened and died. Genl. Cooper, and his son Sam, both appeared to regret my leaving the General's.

Anita: June 8th. *I reached Richmond this evening after a fatiguing ride. My Husband was down to the depot to meet me. I went straight to bed with a sick headache. In my old room on the third story again.*

Monday, 9th. Beautiful day. Great rumors of victories achieved by Jackson in the Valley of Va., are rife to-day, and are credited by all classes. I worked hard at the Office all day. Jackson has whipped Fremont and Shields near Port Republic, Va. Fights on yesterday and to-day.

Saturday, 14th. My wife and I sent Mrs. Myers a set of vases to-day (or rather a pair) for which we gave twenty six dollars—twenty five for vases, and one dollar for freight. Very warm and dry to-day, and two or three days past.

Sunday, 15th. To-day is the anniversary of our wedding—the third year of married life. We went to church in the morning, and heard a Metaphysical sermon from Bishop McGill on the Trinity—this being Trinity Sunday. The sermon was learned, clear, and very beautiful.

It is reported to-day that Stuart, with his Cavalry, has burnt some of the Yankee vessels on the Pamunkey, burnt some of their wagons, destroyed a bridge on the York River Rail Road, run off a number of their horses and mules, and captured one or two hundred prisoners. The weather is extremely warm.

Monday, 16th. Stuart's performance has been brilliant. He entirely flanked McClellan's whole army. He destroyed a hundred wagons, brought in three hundred mules and horses, and came entirely around to the James River side. This will give Genl. Lee most valuable information, and places McClellan in a ridiculous position as a military commander.

Thursday, 26th. Genl. Lee to-day ordered Genl. A.P. Hill's Division across the Chickahominy, via the meadow bridge. Mechanicsville was taken, after a sharp contest, in a most gallant style. Longstreet and Magruder crossed over *via* the Mechanicsville turnpike bridge late in the evening. The cannonading was terrific—that and the volleys of musketry, could distinctly be heard in Richmond. Hundreds of ladies and gentlemen went out to the Northern suberbs [sic] of the City to hear the firing. The bursting of shells, and the flash of the heavy guns could be distinguished very plainly after night fall. The firing ceased a little after nine, P.M. Beautiful day. Great excitement, but still not a sign of disorder, and few, very few, stragglers.

Anita: Thursday, June 26th. This grand battle near Richmond commenced this morning under command of General R. Lee. Gen. Jackson sent in the rear of the enemy. We took Mechanicsville the first day, one of the enemies' best positions.

Friday, 27. The fight was renewed at about half after four, A.M., to-day. The Yankees were driven from one position to another, until darkness closed the contest. We took some strong works, and captured a large number of prisoners. Various rumors were afloat, and most of us were greatly delighted—some croakers there were, who seemed incredulous of any good news—they affected to think McClellan has retreated to entrap us.

Anita: June 27th. The enemy retreated several miles,—it is reported we are whipping them.

Saturday, 28th. Fine weather still. Some eighteen hundred prisoners came up before dinner to-day. Brig. Genl. J.F. Reynolds, Major Clitz, Major Whiting, and other officers of the regular Army amongst them.

Anita: Saturday, June 28th. The battle is progressing favourably to us, I understand. We have captured several thousand prisoners, numbers of officers high in rank.

In the Memoirs of a Southern Belle, Virginia Clay-Clopton (Cousin Jeannie) recorded John Withers' thoughts during this time, and then added an excerpt from a letter he wrote during the terrible Seven Days Battles (a series of six major battles which took place near Richmond over seven days (from June 25 to July 1, 1862)):

"The city is filled with the wounded and dead," echoed our cousin John Withers. "It is fortunate you are away and saved the necessity of beholding the horrible sights which are now so common here! Great numbers of Alabamians are killed and wounded. . . ."

And he added in a letter, written in an interval of the awful Seven Days Battles: "For four days I have been awaiting some decisive move on the part of our forces, but nothing has been done yet to settle affairs. McClellan has not been routed, but his army is, no doubt, demoralised to such an extent as to render any other demonstration against Richmond out of the question for many weeks. . . .The President has come up from the battle-field, and I hear that a courier from the French and British Consuls is to leave here for Washington tonight or in the morning. We will secure between thirty and forty thousand small arms by our late operations; many of them much injured by being bent. The enemy have a position now which we cannot well assail successfully. They are under their gunboats and have gotten reinforcements. . . . There is a report to-night that Magruder has captured eight hundred Yankees to-day, but I place no reliance upon any rumour until it is confirmed as truth. General

Beauregard has made a most successful retreat to Baldwin, thirty-five miles south of Corinth, on the Mobile and Ohio Railroad. The move was necessary, and I have no doubt will be a great blow to the enemy. He carried all his heavy guns, tents, and so on. General Lee is in command of the army hereabouts, and I am sure we will whip McClellan's army when the grand contest shall take place. The rain of last night will forbid any movement for two or three days. When the fight opens again, we will have thousands upon thousands of wounded here!"

Such were the accruing records of woe and of personal and national loss which followed Senator Clay and me throughout those autumn months of '62.

<u>Sunday, 29th.</u> Last night McClellan evacuated his entrenched camp on this side of the Chickahominy and retreated with his whole force towards the James. Magruder had an artillery fight with the rear guard towards night, and killed a great many Yankees, it is said.

<u>Anita: Sunday, June 29th.</u> *The Yankees reported running towards the James River, our forces after them. Everything seems pretty quiet in the city today. I went to Church at ten O'clock this morning. Father Andrews preached.*

<u>Monday, 30th.</u> A severe fight between the Yankees and Genl. A.P. Hill's Division, aided by a portion of Longstreet's Division, took place this afternoon, in which our loss was very heavy, and that of the Yankees believed to be very much

heavier still. We captured Major Genl. G.A. McCall, and Brigadier Genl. Meade. Beautiful weather.

My pay, Capt. Barksdale, was $158.00, and my commutation, Capt. Whitfield, was $35.00.

July, 1862.

<u>Tuesday, 1st.</u> The weather continues to be fine. To-day the body of Mr. Walter Abbott, who was a First Lieutenant in a Company of the 11th Va. Vols., and in command of the Company at the time of his death on the afternoon of yesterday, was brought to Mr. Duval's, his father in law, in the afternoon. His poor wife was terribly shocked, and fainted when she was told of her husband's death. He was shot through the head, the ball entering just over the left eye. We dressed the body and it was placed in a coffin as soon as possible. Mr. Pulaski and Mr. Brown sat up with the corpse.

*<u>Anita: Tuesday July 1st.</u> Mr. Pulaski came in from camp and informed us that poor Mr. Abbot was killed the previous night, soon after this his body was brought to the house in an old wagon covered with straw, he was shot through the head, and of course very much disfigured. No person saw him but the gentlemen. My Husband assisted in dressing and cleaning him. Poor fellow, a nobler heart never lived, he supported his Mother, Wife and child. Little Walter is only thirteen months old. Mrs. Duval has been away during all this **sad** and distressing time, she went to see her Sisters who have lost their two brothers.*

<u>*Wednesday, 2nd.*</u> Raining hard this morning, and continued most of the day. We buried Mr. Abbott about 11, A.M., in the midst of the rain. Nothing special going on to-day.

<u>*Anita: Wednesday, July 2nd.*</u> *Poor Mr. Abbot was buried this morning at 10 O'clock. It was pouring down raining all day long. Mrs. Shober from Salisbury came in to see me, she came to see after her brother's remains, Major Wheat.*

I had a letter from home, poor darling little Maria Gailbeau is dead far away from friends and home, July 3rd, 1862.

Mrs. Col. Chilton also came in to see, she is just down from Danville.

<u>*Thursday, 3rd.*</u> Fine weather again. McClellan and his Army still retreating.

<u>*Friday, 4th.*</u> Beautifully bright day. Anita and I called to see Mrs. Randolph, the wife of the Secretary, and Mrs. Genl. Huger, Mrs. Col. Long, and Mrs. Shober.

<u>*Anita: July 4th.*</u> *No more news from the enemy except that they are still retreating and we pursuing them. The fourth was not celebrated I don't expect by either side. Dr. Brewer and Cousin Tom Adams came in to see me. Mrs. Duval got back home with Miss J. Abbott.*

<u>*Saturday, 5th.*</u> Nothing special going on to-day. Fine weather.

<u>*Sunday, 6th.*</u> Lovely day. I went to church in the morning, and heard a fine sermon from Bishop McGill: a doctrinal sermon

on the parable of the fishermen letting down their nets and taking great multitudes of fish. The application the bishop made was that our Savior taught from Peter's ship—that Peter was the rock on which the church was built—that no other than the Catholic church is the true ship, rock or church. He preached nearly an hour.

Thursday, 10th. Genl. Winder left Mrs. Duval's to-day, and moved up to the corner of Franklin and 2nd. Streets. Rained some to-day.

Anita: July 9th. The day has been oppressively hot. I walked to the city spring in the evening after Tea.

Thursday 10th. Very warm all the morning, but we had a delightful shower by evening that cooled the atmosphere—Mrs. Williams has gotten back from Charlotte, we went round to see her last night at Mrs. Nelson's. General Winder has left this house.

July 11th. Friday. A cool and pleasant day. I am still working at my tuck skirt, it will look very pretty when it is done up—

Saturday—We moved downstairs to our old room this morning. Capt. Myers came in to see us, he came to the city on business.

Saturday, 12th. Fine day. Genl. Lee has moved his Hd. Qrs. back to Dobb's House, on the nine mile, or stony run road, 2 ½ miles from the City. The whole Army has been brought back to the lines occupied before the fight. Anita and I moved down to-day to the room on the first floor at Mrs. Duval's which we occupied before Anita went to N.C. Capt. Myers is up here from Salisbury.

<u>Sunday, 13th.</u> Anita and I went to Church in the morning, and heard a sermon from the Bishop on the virtue of charity. Fine weather.

<u>Anita: Monday 14th.</u> *I finished my skirt. I sang in the choir this morning, practising to sing a requiem Mass for Mrs. McNulty. Mrs. Stuart played the organ. In the evening we went round to Mrs. Maury's and spent the evening. I also called on Miss Blake and Mrs. Anderson.*

<u>Tuesday 15th</u>. *Today is a very hot day. I walked out to Church at eight o'clock. About 1 O'clock The Capt. came home and brought Gen. Hood with him, they took a drink and a little lunch. Capt. Myers came in also. We had a delightful shower in the evening—We remained at home.*

We heard that poor old General Twiggs died today in Augusta, Georgia.

<u>Thursday 17th.</u> *I wrote a letter to Cousin Jeannie about getting Mrs. Abbott some Bombazine.*

<u>Saturday 19th.</u> *A cool day. I called on Mrs. Thomas—We called on Mrs. Davis.*

<u>Sunday, 20th.</u> The past week was not characterized by anything unusual around Richmond. It is said that a full arrangement has been entered into between the Yankee

Government and our own for a mutual exchange of prisoners. We have lately had successes in Tennessee and Kentucky by our partizan rangers and regular cavalry. Forrest has captured Murfreesboro, Tenn., and Morgan has gotten into the heart of Kentucky. A great panic prevails in the North.

To-day is the anniversary of the death of our dear baby: we went to church in the morning. Fine weather.

Anita: Sunday 20th. We went to Church and heard a French priest preach an excellent sermon. In the evening we went to Mrs. Nelson's.

Monday, 21st. To-day is the anniversary of the battle of Manassas. Anita and I took tea at Mr. James Purcell's. Deshler took dinner with us: he had not seen us here since just a year ago.

Anita: Monday 21st. Mr. Niendoff and Mr. Snowdon came to see me today. Mr. N. returns to Texas tomorrow, I write to my Mother by him — In the evening we went to Mrs. James Purcell's.

Tuesday, 22nd. I have to-day received from the President the appointment of Lt. Col. in the Adjutant Genl. Department of the Provisional Army, to take rank from January 1st, 1862. Cousin Thomas Adams spent the evening with us. Fine day.

Anita: Tuesday 22nd. Rather warm. John Elliot called to see me.

My Husband was made a Lt. Colonel today which will date from January last. I am thinking about going to the Springs next week with Mrs. Branch.

<u>Wednesday, 23rd.</u> Mrs. Duval, Anita and I rode out to Mr. Pulaski's after dinner, and did not get back until half after nine, P.M. Anita has been quite unwell all day with sick headache. Rained a little in the afternoon. Major Palfrey, Asst. Adjt. Genl., Provisional Army, has been assigned to duty in the Office at my request: he is a graduate of West Point.

<u>Saturday, 26th.</u> Nothing special the past three days—weather good. Rained this afternoon, and at night.

To-day I drew my back pay from January 1st., 1862 to June 30th., 1862, (that is the difference between my pay as a Captain and Lieutenant Colonel) from Capt. Barksdale, A.Q.M. The amount was two hundred and seventy dollars ($270). My back commutation for the same period, on same account, which was paid me by Captain Whitfield, A.Q.M., was seventy one dollars and fifty cents, (71.50). The whole amount of my back pay was, therefore, ($341.50), three hundred and forty one dollars and fifty cents. This will help me along very considerably: my expenses for boarding have nearly doubled of late, although I am at the same place and have no more room than heretofore.

<u>Sunday, 27th.</u> Anita and I went to church in the morning. Fine weather.

Anita: Monday, July 28th. The Capt. had a letter from Cousin Lawson, he and Mr. Tracy have been recommended for Brigadiers. I called on Mrs. Gen. Cooper yesterday, they seemed glad to get back to Richmond.

I am packing to go to the Springs tomorrow with Mr. Bulkley and Mrs. Branch. Poor old Dr. Curtis died this morn—and will be buried tomorrow at Pacoose.

Wednesday, 30th. Very warm yesterday, and to-day. Rained early this morning, then cleared up, and rained again at night.

Thursday, 31st. Mrs. William's father, Dr. Curtis, breathed his last about five O'Clock this morning. Rained hard in afternoon. My pay this month, as Lieut. Col., Capt. Hutter, A.Q.M., was $203.00, and my commutation, Capt. Whitfield, was $47.00. This, with my back pay from January 1st., to June 30th., $270.00, and my back commutation for same period, $71.50, both of which I drew on the 26th. Instant, make my pay this month amount to $591.50.

August, 1862.

Friday, 1st. My wife left here for the Alleghany Springs this morning, in company with Mrs. Branch, and Mr. and Mrs. Bulckley—Charlotte went along with Anita. Beautiful day.

Dr. Curtis, Mrs. William's father, was buried out at his late farm, about eight miles from the City.

We have news to-day that some of our Artillery attacked McClellan's fleet last night after midnight, and it is surmised that great damage was done. It took place from Coggin's point, opposite McClellan's camp.

Anita: Friday, August 1st. We started for the Springs this morning, had a most disagreeable time, very much crowded until we got to Lynchburg. Mrs. Branch and myself both went to bed with dreadful sick headaches.

Saturday, 2nd. Major Whiting, A.A. Genl., Provisional Army, went on duty in the Office to-day. This will relieve me greatly. He is to be in Genl. Cooper's room, where Col. Chilton formerly was. Fine weather—cloudy towards night.

Anita: Saturday, August 2nd. We reached the Alleghany about one O'clock, very much fatigued. We were all put in one large room, sixteen of us, the place is **so** dreadfully crowded.

Sunday, 3rd. Very warm and showery. I went to church in the morning, and heard a good sermon from the Bishop on the giving an account of our stewardships. Wrote to Anita this afternoon.

Anita: Sunday, 3rd. I have met a few acquaintances—The fare is only torable [sic]. Cousin Edmund is here, he stays a good deal with us. I wrote to my Husband today.

Monday, 4th. Very warm all day, and in the evening. Caldwell and I called at Mrs. Nelson's after tea, and then took a long walk. I was very busy at the Office all day long.

Anita: Monday 4th. It is very warm today. I have taken one of Mrs. Morris's rooms for a while. They had dancing last evening. I went into the room for a little while.

Tuesday, August 5th. The day is intensely warm—the nights cool.

Thursday, 7th. Weather still intensely warm. Mrs. Cochrane, (Billy Beall's Sister) and her grown daughter Miss Ada, got here yesterday, having run the blockade from Fredericksburg. They came to see me this morning, and wanted to find where their brother was.

Friday, 8th. Major Whiting, Mr. Branch, Mr. Caldwell and I rode down in a carriage to Drewry's Bluff in the afternoon:

the weather was intensely hot. We saw Captain Smith Lee, of the Navy, who is in command at Drewry's, Capt. Chetard, Capt. Barney, and Capt. Tucker, C.S. Navy, and other gentlemen who are stationed there. They kindly had us shown all around, and were otherwise very polite and attentive to us. We had a most agreeable visit, and returned so as to reach the City by ten, P.M. The works at Drewry's look as if they were impregnable to any Naval attack, and will be very difficult to reduce by a combined land and naval attack.

Saturday, 9th. Mrs. Cochrane and Miss Ada, failing in the attempt to get rooms elsewhere, to-day came to Mrs. Duval's and accepted my room—I moved up to Mr. Branch's, and took part of his bed.

Anita: Saturday, 9th. We have been here a week today. I like the place very well. I have made a great many pleasant acquaintances. Cousin Edmund has left me. I wrote to my dear Husband today.

Sunday, 10th. I went to church in the morning. The Bishop gave us a very good sermon. Not many persons present—or rather not so many as usual. Weather intensely hot until about 5 ½ P.M., when we had a shower of rain accompanied by a breeze which was truly refreshing.

*Anita: Sunday, 10th. A very warm day. Mrs. Morris has been **so** good and kind to me. Mrs. Branch and Mr. Bulkley speak of going away next week—I don't think I shall accompany them.*

August 13th-19th. Mrs. Branch and party left the Alleghany on Wednesday 13th.

I moved to No. 51 Thursday. Lucy Fontaine roomed with me for a few days.

I was taken sick on Tuesday 19th. I believe I had a slight chill and fever all the evening—remained in my room several days. Dr. Morris came to see his family last week, Mary was sick. Mr. Cranz sent me a little brandy.

<u>Friday, 15th.</u> The weather has been pleasant this week. Mr. Caldwell left for Texas yesterday. A great many troops are leaving here to join Jackson's command: they go up by the central cars.

<u>Saturday, 16th.</u> Robert Brown and I rode out to Mr. Pulaski's, about 6 miles North East of the City, late in the afternoon, and stayed all night. Delightful weather.

<u>Sunday, 17th.</u> Mrs. Pulaski, Mrs. Harney (a lady visitor) and I went to church in the forenoon: the country church is the same at which Mr. Wilmer, now Bishop of Alabama, used to Officiate. We heard a tolerable sermon from Mr. Walker, formerly of Alexandria. Brown and I returned to the City in the afternoon—having had a most charming visit. Cousin Clement and Cousin Jeannie were at Mrs. Winn's when we returned—having arrived by the afternoon train from Lynchburg.

<u>Monday, 18th.</u> Lovely weather still. Beautiful days, and nights just cool enough to enjoy a blanket. Congress met to-day—a quorum in both branches was present. The President's message was read, and the two houses adjourned.

<u>*Tuesday, 19th.*</u> Fine day. Troops still passing through, en route to join Genl. Lee at Gordonsville. McClellan has certainly abandoned his positions, on both sides of the James, which he lately occupied some thirty miles below this city.

<u>*Anita: Thursday. August 21st.*</u> *Many of my friends left today. Mrs. and Miss Fontaine and Mrs. Ruffin. I moved again to Mrs. Ruffin's old room. I am very well pleased with it.*

I wrote to my Husband yesterday that I was sick. All my friends have been very kind to me here.

<u>*Saturday, 23rd.*</u> Cousin Virginia spent the day at Mrs. Duval's: Cousin Clement came down and took tea—they went home soon after tea. Quite warm to-day. Rained quite hard a little while after dark. Yesterday I received a letter from my dear wife saying she had been right sick for a day or two, and feared she had had a chill. This evening I received another telling me she was very well again. Last night I received a box of fruit by express, but have not as yet gotten any letter telling me to whom I am indebted for so nice a present. I rather expect that my friend Captain Myers has laid me under his additional obligation.

<u>*Anita: Saturday, 23rd.*</u> *We have two splendid singers here, Miss Cabell and Mrs. Lee. Today I feel much better—Rather cloudy. I think we shall have rain.*

<u>*Sunday, 24th.*</u> Heard the bishop preach in the morning: no music. Wrote to Anita, and Mrs. Gov. Bell, after church. Dined at Mr. John Purcell's—he has lately returned from a two months

trip up the country. Beautiful day. Several of us went with Capt. Maynard out to call on Mr. Cowardin late in the afternoon.

Monday, 25th. I to-day received a box from Raleigh, N.C., per express, which has been on the way since the 9th. Inst. It contained a little keg of whiskey, a present from my friend Cap. W.W. Pierce, A.Q.M. Fine day.

Wednesday, 27th. Left Richmond in the morning, at 8 O'Clock, and reached Lynchburg at 6 ½ P.M. Met a brother of Jno. M. Jones' on the way, and put up at the Cabell House with him. Met several acquaintances in the City.

Thursday, 28th. Left Lynchburg about daylight, and got to the Alleghany Springs at 12 ½ O'Clock in the day. Found my wife very well.

Anita: Thursday, 28th. My Husband arrived today quite unexpectedly. I was mighty glad to see him. A delightful day it is.

Friday, 29th.-Saturday, 30th. Spent these two days most delightfully. Beautiful weather, lovely place, good fare, and with my dear wife—I was as happy as I could expect to be.

Anita: Friday, 29th. A pleasant day. We have nice dancing now since the Capt. came to see me. Mrs. Cranz, Kent Fishbourne and myself.

Saturday, 30th. A great many persons left today. Mrs. McDaniel, Mrs. Sutton and all that party. My husband had a letter from Major

Whiting today, he will have to return to Richmond tomorrow, Sunday.

<u>Sunday, 31st.</u> Left the Alleghany Springs at one, P.M., and reached Lynchburg after dark. Stayed at the Piedmont House—miserable hotel, full of rats.

<u>*Anita: Sunday, 31st.*</u> *My Husband is getting ready to leave torectly [sic]. All have all gone up to the house to [sic] preaching. Mr. Wilmer is going to preach.*

We had a letter from my brother the other day, he says he is going to get married very soon to Miss Annette Magoffin.

My Husband left me on Sunday, 31st. of August.

*A **Grand** battle fought at Manassas on that day, Gen. Lee in command.*

We came to Coyner's on the 2nd. of September—spent a few days rather pleasantly. T. came with Mr. Webb and Mr. Harrison of Richmond.

My pay this month was $203.00, and my commutation, Capt. J. F. Whitfield, was $73.00.

September, 1862.

<u>Monday, 1st.</u> I came down from Lynchburg to Richmond to-day. Genl. and Mrs. J.E. Johnston got on the cars at Jetersville, the depot for the Amelia Springs, and came down with me. The General's general health appears to be very good.

<u>Anita: Sep. 4th.</u> *We have Dancing every evening, but it is very quiet in comparison to the Alleghany — there are very few persons here now. I wrote to my sister Maria and to Grandpapa by Mr. Ferguson, who is ordered there by our Government.*

<u>Sept. 6th.</u> *The weather has been very cool up here until the last day or two.*

<u>Sunday, 7th.</u> The weather has been beautiful the past week. The week has been an eventful one. Genl. Lee, having whipped McClellan's and Pope's combined armies at Manassas on the 30th Ult., and Genl. Kirby Smith having whipped Nelson's Army at Richmond, Ky., our armies have this week been advancing upon the enemy. The greater portion of Genl. Lee's Army has entered Maryland, and Kirby Smith has moved up towards Cincinnati. Our prospects are brighter now than they have been during the war.

I went to church in the morning, and heard the Bishop on the subject of confession and penance: the text was from the parable of the ten lepers who were cleansed and directed by our Savior to go show themselves to the Priests—only one of whom returned to give thanks to Jesus, who had healed them. I dined with Mr. John Purcell. Mrs. Purcell returned home yesterday.

Monday, 8th. Beautiful weather—lovely, moonlight nights. We hear that the Yankees have evacuated North Alabama, and portions of Tennessee. Bragg is after them.

Anita: Sept. 8th. I received two letters from my Husband today, and one he sent me from my Uncle Tom.

The day is very, warm— I expect to start for Richmond tomorrow about twelve O'clock.

Tuesday, Sept. 9th. We left Coyners today, we have had quite a pleasant time there— We met Mrs. Cranz at the depot, she will go to Richmond with us—by Charlottesville—

We arrived in Rich— on Wednesday—about 5 O'clock—my Husband met me at the depot all seemed glad to see me—

Wednesday, 10th. Anita returned from the springs in the afternoon, by the central train, having come from Lynchburg, via Charlottesville. She is much improved by the trip. We have extravagant rumors to the effect that Kirby Smith has captured Cincinnati, and other wonderful things.

Friday, 12th. Rained a little to-night. Very close and warm all the afternoon. Rumored that Baltimore has been surrendered to the Confederate Army. Genl. Lee writes encouragingly of the feeling in Maryland and says our Confederate currency is taken by the people in payment for supplies—this is much better than the people of Kentucky did last year. In the latter State we had to pay gold for supplies, notwithstanding the State had Senators and Representatives in our Congress, and had been regularly admitted as one of the Confederate States. I trust greatly in the loyalty of Maryland.

Saturday, 13th. No news to-day from our armies. Two thousand five hundred Yankee prisoners left here yesterday on their return home paroled and exchanged. I dined with Capt. Maynard to-day.

Anita: Saturday, Sept. 13th. Cousin Clement came to see us and took breakfast with us. Cousin Jeannie is gone to N. Carolina.

Sunday, 14th. Anita and I went to church in the morning. Beautiful day. Father Mullen preached: no music. The Bishop is absent from the City on a few days visit to the springs. I dined at Mr. Purcell's. After dinner Capt. Maynard took us out to Mechanicsville and Beaver Dam.

Anita: Monday, 15th. My Husband went to the battle field with Mr. Purcell and Menard and spent the day riding about. I called on Mrs. Morris and Mrs. Purcell.

Tuesday, 16th. Took breakfast with Capt. Maynard at Mr. Purcell's. After breakfast we started on a trip to the battlefields.

Mr. John Purcell, John Cowardin, Capt. Maynard and I went to Mechanicsville, Beaver Dam, Ellyson's Mill, Gaines' Mill, near Coal Harbor, across the Woodbury road or grape vine bridge road, down to Savage's Station, and up by Fair Oaks. We called in at Mr. Joe Randolph's on our return, and got back to the city about seven, P.M. We had a most charming day of it. My face was worse sun burnt than any of the party. We took lunch along, and enjoyed our mid-day repast more than we would fine dinner at home.

Anita: Tuesday 16th. *A warm day—We've had a fight at Harper's ferry—*

Wednesday, 17th. It is reported to-day that Genl. Lee has captured Harper's Ferry, and eight thousand prisoners. Anita and I spent the evening with Cousin Clement and Cousin Jeannie—the latter just returned here from North Carolina the day before yesterday.

Anita: Wednesday 17th. *I went to Mrs. Wimes to spend the evening with Cousin Jeannie— We had a pleasant time, they made me play and sing— Gen. and Mrs. Johnston were very cordial—*

Tuesday, 18th. To-day having been set apart by the President as one of thanksgiving, the business houses and public offices were closed, and services held in the various churches. Anita and I went to church at ten, A.M. The weather has been beautiful this week—it is very warm to-day.

Anita: Thursday. Sept. 18th.   *Thanksgiving Day. We went to Church, but had no sermon—a very warm day— Gen. E. Jones and Major Williams called to see us in the evening.*

Friday, 19th. An exceedingly **hot** *day—Mrs. Gen. Joe Johnston called to see Mrs. Whiting and myself. Mrs. Walker came on Friday, Sept. 26th.*

Sunday, 28th. Fine weather the past ten days, and beautiful to-day. Anita and I went with a party to Drewry's Bluff last Wednesday. To-day we went to church at ten, A.M., and heard Father Mullen. Mrs. Genl. Walker (Sophia Baylor) arrived here from N.C., the night before last, and is stopping at Mrs. Duval's. Cousin Jeannie spent the day with Anita yesterday, and Cousin Clement dined with us. Mr. Baylor, the free trade man, spent the evening at Mrs. Duval's—he is a very plausible and interesting man.

Tuesday, 30th. Beautiful weather. My pay this month, Captain Hutter, A.Q.M., was $203.00, and my commutation, Maj. J.F. Whitfield, A.Q.M., was $74.00.

October, 1862.

Anita: October 1st. Mrs. Walker, Mrs. Whiting and myself went visiting— it is a very warm sultry day—

Saturday, 4th. Fine weather. Nothing special going on.

Anita: Sunday, Oct. 5th. We had a letter from Joe yesterday in which he mentioned he expected to be married on the 4th. day of September.

Monday, 6th. We went round to Mrs. Winder's to spend the evening—the night was beautiful.

Saturday, 11th. Rained to-day for the first time in some weeks, with the exception of a warm shower yesterday. Turned cool to-day.

Sunday, 12th. Cold and damp all day—dark night.

Monday, 13th. Congress adjourned to-day. Rainy and cold. We had fire in the parlor, during the afternoon and evening, for the first time this Fall. I went up to see Cousin Clement and Cousin Jeannie in the evening—Cousin Clement called to see us in the afternoon.

Tuesday, 14th. Cloudy and damp to-day, but milder than yesterday. Nothing special going on. Cousin Jeannie came to see Anita this morning.

Anita, Sunday, 19th. I went to Church, we had a fine sermon from the Bishop. After Church we went to Mr. James & John Purcell's. We dined at the latter's. In the afternoon Miss Lizzie and myself went to Church, a strange priest preached. We went to Mrs. Smith's little girl's funeral on Tuesday 21st. she was burnt to death.

Sunday, 26th. It is raining today. My Husband would not let me go to Church.

Friday, 31st. Fine weather for some weeks. Poor Aaron Cohen, who was our first messenger at Montgomery died a few days since of inflammation of the stomach.

My pay, Capt. Hutter, was $203.00, and my commutation, Maj. Whitfield, was $112.50.

November, 1862.

<u>Saturday, 1st.</u> Nothing special going on.

<u>Anita: November 1st.</u> *Feast of All Saints. I went to Church at ten O'clock, and did intend to go to communion but did go. In the afternoon I went to see Mrs. Doherty, Dollie O'Reilly that was, and had a long chat with her about Nazareth girls— In the evening I went around to Mrs. Nelson's. I missed my———this months of Oct.*

<u>Sunday, 2nd.</u> Spent the day at Mr. Grant's, a few miles in the country from Richmond. Jno. Purcell, Maynard and a few others of us had a most agreeable day. Old Mr. Goddin 82 years of age, and Mr. Dill, 72 years of age, were with us, and contributed greatly to the amusement of all present by their jokes on each other. I called to see Genl. Lee when I returned to the City.

<u>Anita: Monday, Nov. 3rd.</u> *I went out to see poor Mrs. Menard, she look [sic] wretchedly thin and sick, still quite cheerful—and resigned to die I think.*

Wednesday, 5th. Genl. Lee, Genl. Bragg, and Genl. E.K. Smith, have all been here within the past ten days, but have all left now. Rained this evening.

Anita, Wednesday, 5th. Dr. Dean came to see me. I did not go out, it rained a little today.

Thursday--it rained and was disagreeable and windy.

Thursday, 6th. Quite cool and damp all day.

Friday, 7th. When we awoke this morning we found, to our amazement, that the country was covered with snow. Snow continued to fall nearly all day, but melted in the streets almost as fast as it fell. Joe Dwyer, my wife's brother, got here early this morning. We are perfectly delighted to see him, and especially to see him looking so well. He is one of the finest looking men to be found.

Anita: Friday, 7th. A heavy fall of snow fell. My brother Joe, to my great surprise, came to see me to take me home—he look very stout and in fine health and spirits.

Saturday, 8th. It stopped snowing. Joe and myself made a few calls.

Sunday, 9th. Joe, Anita and I went to church in the morning. We dined at home. The snow is melted, and the weather much milder.

Anita: Sunday, 9th. *Joe, myself and the Capt. went to Church—heard a good sermon from a french priest on sin. In the afternoon I went to Benediction. After Church we called to see the Bishop.*

Thursday, 13th. The weather this week has been fine. Joe and Anita, and Joe and I, have visited most of our friends in the City this week. Genl. Polk, and Genl. Heth are here from Bragg's Army. It is believed now that Genl. Joe Johnston is to go to Tennessee to take command of Bragg's Army.

Anita: Sunday, 16th. *I went to Holy communion early this morning. Joe and the Capt. went to Church at 11 O'clock. Father McMullen preached rather a poor sermon. In the afternoon I went to Vespers, the Bishop preached.*

Monday, 17th. *We went round to see Dr. and Mrs. Wayt, she begged us to stay for all day, we had a nice dinner, they were all very kind to me.*

Tuesday, 18th. *It rained, and so it continued all the rest of the week. Joe went up to Gen. Lee's Army—I feel badly nearly all the time.*

Saturday, 22nd. *This morning we went down to see the Gunboat Richmond. Joe's brothers-in-law have arrived here. Gen. Sibley is soon expected—*

Sunday, 23rd. Anita and I went to church in the morning, but I had to leave to make room for some ladies. We dined at James Purcell's. Joe is still here. Mrs. Walker left here last Wednesday—she goes to Marietta, Georgia, to remain with her mother, and the General goes to the trans-Mississippi to report to Genl. Holmes. Beautiful day. Weather right cold.

Sunday, 30th. Anita, Joe and I went to church in the morning, and dined at home. Pleasant day.

Anita: Sunday, 30th. *The Capt. Joe and myself went to Church. Father Hagen preached. A beautiful day.*

Monday--I wrote home.

My pay this month, Capt. Barksdale, was $203.00, and my commutation, Major Whitfield, was $123.00.

December, 1862.

<u>Monday, 1st.</u> Nothing of special interest transpiring. Weather quite moderate for the season.

<u>Anita: 1st. Dec.</u> *Tuesday evening the Capt. and Joe went to Mr. Davis's, the President, had a cup of Tea.*

<u>Thursday, 4th.</u> Fine day—pretty frosty in the morning and at night. Small pox reported to be spreading in the City. Anita and I were vaccinated by Dr. Brewer this morning. Joe Dwyer left for San Antonio by the Lynchburg train at six O'Clock in the afternoon.

<u>Anita: Thursday, 4th. December.</u> *Joe had his likeness taken. He left us and started for Texas. I wish we could have gone with him.*

<u>Friday, 5th.</u> *It rained all day long, we could not stir out of the house.*

<u>Saturday, 6th.</u> *A cold day. I went to Mrs. Allen's to see about Mrs. Myers bonnet, it was finished and quite pretty, like a perfectly new bonnet. I called on Mr. Harrison and Mrs. Nelson and Maury. Mrs. Whiting sister Nora came today—also Mrs. Govan and Jimmy Duval. The [sic] is crowded now.*

Sunday, 7th. Very cold last night and to-day: the water in the hall hydrant has been frozen all day. Clear and bright. Anita and I went to church in the morning, and remained at home the rest of the day.

Anita: Sunday 7th. We went to Church at 11 O'clock — The Bishop gave us a splendid sermon on Miracles.

Wednesday, December 10th. I have a wretched cold in my head. I took a walk in the morning — it is a beautiful day.

I have just heard of the death of poor Mrs. Menard, one of the sweetest women in the world.

I went to bed at four O'clock feeling very badly. My Husband went to dine round to Judge Crump's, I was sorry I could not accompany him. Cousin Edmund is quite sick also.

Thursday, 11th. Beautiful weather. Abolition Army began the passage of the Rappahannock to-day. Three pontoon bridges were thrown across — one at Fredericksburg, and two below. The enemy occupied Fredericksburg by night time.

Anita: Thursday, 11th. Mrs. Menard was buried this morning at 11 O'clock. I went to the Church but it was so intensely cold I could not stand it, I had to leave. Dr. Dean came to see me today. I had a letter from sister Sue urging me to go and pay them a visit.

Friday, 12th. Fine day. Enemy crossing the Rappahannock on their bridges all last night and to-day, under cover of their guns which are posted on the North bank. Anita went over to

Petersburg to-day, to make a little visit to Cousin Thomas Withers. Cousin Edmund went with her. Whiting, Palfrey and I went up and took some roasted oysters and real coffee with Maj. A.D. Banks in the evening. Mr. Davis, our worthy President, left here two or three days since on a short visit to Mississippi. Brig. Genl. Joe Davis went with him.

Anita: Friday, 12th. I went over to Petersburg with cousin Edmund in the evening. The Capt. went over Saturday, remained until Monday with us. I had a very nice time, enjoyed myself in a quiet way — had a splendid appetite, liked the crackling bread particularly well. Mrs. Hinton was very kind to me, invited me to stay with her. Mrs. Brooks and Miss Dunn called on me. I returned home on Thursday evening with Cousin Edmund. I had a letter from Sophie and one from Mrs. Myers asking me to go and spend Christmas with her.

Saturday, 13th. Burnside attacked Genl. Lee at Fredericksburg to-day, and was repulsed at all points. Genl. T.R.R. Cobb, on our side, was killed, and Genl. Maxcy Gregg badly wounded. Beautiful day. I went to Petersburg.

Sunday, 14th. Very mild. Anita went to church with Mrs. Hinton. Dr. Dunn and I took a long buggy ride. Very little fighting in Genl. Lee's army to-day. Genl. Evans, near Kinston, N.C., had a brush on yesterday with Genl. Foster's Yankee forces and held them in check.

Monday, 15th. I returned to Richmond in the morning. Genl. G.W. Smith, who went to Petersburg Saturday, went to Goldsboro, N.C., this morning with his staff.

Anita: Friday, Dec. 19. We have again whipped the Yankees at Fredericksburg. They are fighting also at Kingston, in N. Carolina.

Friday 19th. Major Whiting was taken sick. I went out in the morning to see some of my friends.

Saturday — It was bitter cold — I went visiting.

Sunday, 21st. Fine weather still. Bitter cold yesterday and to-day. Anita and I went to church in the morning.

Anita: Sunday, 21st. We went to Church late. After Church we had a meeting of the ladies. They are organizing a society for the Relief of the poor. We had a nice dinner today.

Monday, 22nd. Dr. Talley and his brother started home this morning, the Dr. quite unwell.

Major is quite sick, Dr. Talley says he has scarlet fever.

Wednesday, 24th. Christmas eve. Major Whiting is dangerously ill. Dr. Dunn and Dr. Peachy are attending him —

Thursday, 25th. This is a lovely Christmas day, and thousands in this city, and elsewhere, are enjoying it to the full. Our household, however, at Mrs. Duval's have been rendered sad beyond expression by the death of Major Jasper S. Whiting, Asst. Adjt. Genl., who breathed his last at ten minutes before four O'Clock, A.M. He was taken ill last Friday night, the 19th. Inst., of what proved to be malignant scarlet fever. He was buried, at the request of the physician, Dr. Peachey, at four

O'Clock this afternoon. He was buried with Military honors in the beautiful cemetery near this city.

Mr. Minnigerode, rector of St. Paul's Episcopal Church, offici-ated—the funeral taking place from his church, of which Major Whiting was a member. Mrs. Whiting is almost heart broken, and we are all deeply grieved at this sad bereavement.

Anita: Christmas morning at four O'clock Major Whiting died, his wife came down and asked my Husband to go up—when he got there the poor man had expired—he was delerious [sic] during his whole sickness—

Christmas day I went to Church at half past ten. My Husband was busy and could not go—he had to attend to every thing for Mrs. Whiting, her husband had to be buried the same afternoon—

It was the saddest Christmas I ever spent—no person dined out, though many were invited. We were to have dined at Mr. John Pur-cell's.

Friday, 26th. I went up to see Mrs. Whiting, it excited me a good deal—I felt very badly all day. Mrs. Doherty and myself went round to see the Bishop. By night I felt quite sick, dreadful pains in my limbs. My Husband went round to Major Williams to drink Egg-Nogg, Mrs. Govan and Mrs. Abbott sat with me until ten O'clock.

Saturday, 27th. To-day Captain Jno. C. Maynard and I went out to the cemetery and had Major Whiting's body removed to Capt. Maynard's private enclosure in the cemetery. Warm to-day. Sprinkled rain a little most of the day, and rained a good deal towards night, and after night. My dear wife was quite sick last night, and has been in bed all day: the Doctor, Dr. Dean, says she has taken a slight cold.

Anita: Saturday, 27th. I was sick in bed all day, Dr. Dean came to see me. Mrs. Whiting went over to Mrs. Ives this morning.

Sunday, 28th. I went to church in the morning—Anita was too weak to go out. I called at Mr. Jno. Purcell's after tea.

Monday, 29th. I called to see Genls. Hood and Chilton, and Col. Long, in the afternoon.

Anita: Monday, 29th. I am much better today. It is a most lovely day. In the afternoon my Husband and myself went for Mrs. W. and took her to see her Husband's grave.

Tuesday, 30th. I have not felt very well for the past two or three days. My hands and feet have been perspiring day and night. This morning I spat up bile three or four times. I have been very moderate in my diet for a couple of days. My back hurts me a little.

Wednesday, 31st. My pay this month, Capt. Barksdale, was $203.00, and my commutation, Major Whitfield, was $130.00.

End of Lt. Col. Withers' Journal.

January, 1863.

Anita's Diary (January, 1863-September, 1865).

<u>New Year's day, Jan'y 1st. Thursday.</u> *Was a most lovely day. I felt perfectly miserable, as sick as I could be. My Husband took me out riding in the afternoon, Mrs. Govan went with us. Dr. Dean came to see me in the evening—he would not give me any medicine but told me to go out all the time—*

<u>Friday, Jan. 2nd.</u> *I am better, walked out to see Mrs. Whiting this morn, told her farewell. I went to see Mrs. Maury, she begged me to stay and spend the day, which I did,—she proposed my going up to see Mrs. Wayt, which I think I will do. I wrote to my Mother by Mr. Pierce.*

<u>Sunday, 4th.</u> *We went to church at half past eight—I got sick and had to leave. My Husband breakfasted at Mr. J. Purcell's—after that they went out to the country and spent the day at Mr. Grant's. I spent the day with the ladies, had a nice dinner. In the afternoon went to Church and confession. Mr. Menard walked home with me.*

<u>January 5th.</u> *My birthday, I am 24 years old today. I went to Holy communion early this morning. I came home quite sick— My*

Husband gave me a nice large cake and apples. I am going to Dr. Wayt's farm tomorrow.

Tuesday, 6th. Bettie Greenhow and myself started for Dr. Wayt's — when we reached there it was raining. Bettie had a headache. They were all glad to see us.

Wednesday, 7th. Not a very fine day. I had a sick head ache all day, I did not even go down to breakfast, I could not retain a thing in my stomach all day.

Thursday, 8th. I was a little better. Mrs. Wayt is so comfortably fixed.

Friday, 9th. Miss Jeannie Abbot and Miss Bouldin came over to see us, the former teaches in the country. I am better today. I enjoy everything so much.

Saturday, 10th. It rained awfully all day. My Husband came over, — we had an elegant dinner.

Sunday, 11th. We did not go to Church — we took a pleasant drive before dinner.

Monday, 12th. My Husband returned to town. We had a beautiful day. Friday we returned, they all thought that I had improved.

Monday, 19th. I made several visits in the morning. We went to Mr. Maury's and took Tea. Tuesday, Wednesday and Thursday it rained all day. Feb. 25th. Capt. and Mr. Purcell and Palfrey went out to Mr. Grant's.

February, 1863.

<u>Sunday, Feb. 8th.</u> We went to Church at 8 ½. My husband has gone to dine with Charles Purcell—and cousin Lawson. Cousin Clement and Lawson stay here. Captain Myers is going to dine with me.

<u>Tuesday, 10th.</u> Mrs. Semmes gave a delightful party. We enjoyed it very much, we met all the elite of Richmond there.

<u>Tuesday, 17th.</u> Mrs. George Randolph gave a party. I could not go it was raining **so** hard. The Capt. went and found it quite pleasant.

<u>Wednesday, 18th.</u> Ash Wed. It was raining and I could not go to Church—

I will not be able to fast this Lent—

<u>Sunday, 22nd.</u> My Husband's birthday. I had nothing to give him. It has been snowing heavily all day long. I could not get to Church.

I had my mouseline dress dyed for $2. and made it up myself. 23—24 —25th.

March, 1863.

<u>March 1st. Sunday.</u> We went to Church at 11ven. Father Mac preached—from we went to Mr. John Purcell's to dine, it cleared off and is quite mild today. Mr. James Grant came to see us.

<u>Monday, March 2nd.</u> A bright beautiful day, I made several calls— In the evening Dr. and Mrs. Talley and ourselves went to the President's—met Dr. and Mrs. Garnet there—we had a pleasant evening.

<u>Wednesday, 4th.</u> A bitter cold day. Mrs. Tally and myself made some visits. In the evening Capt. went to Mrs. Nelson's to spend the evening. Dr. and Mrs. Wayt are down from the country. I did not go because it was **too cold**. Judge Crump called to see us and Cousin Clement.

<u>Thursday, 5th.</u> I spent the day at Mrs. Nelson's, had a nice dinner. Went to Church in the afternoon. In the evening we went to a party at Dr. Morris's--we had a pleasant time. Some of the ladies danced.

<u>Friday, 6th.</u> I feel pretty well today. I took my breakfast in my room, had a nice cup of chocolate. A cold, windy day—I can't go out. Mrs. Duval has raised the board to a hundred dollars.

Thursday, 13th. Cousin Tom Adams — John Grammer came to see us in the evening. Capt. went to call on the Misses Preston.

Saturday — I went to Petersburg — we had very cold weather.

Sunday we went to Church. Father Mulby gave us a stirring sermon. — 15th.

I spent a very pleasant week in Petersburg — We had a heavy fall of snow, which prevented my returning to Richmond on the day I appointed. Mrs. Hinton invited us to dine with her, she is a nice, agreeable little woman.

Saturday, 21st. My Husband to my great surprise came over to Petersburg.

Sunday, 22nd. The Capt. went out to the country with Cousin Tom. I went to Church in all the snow.

Monday, 23rd. We returned to Richmond, father Huber came over with us.

Wednesday, 25th. Feast of the Annunciation. I went to Church, after that Mrs. James Purcell and myself went to see Mrs. Cranz who is going to Europe, also Mrs. John Purcell.

Thursday it rained all day.

Friday — a day of fasting and prayer. We went to Church at nine O'clock — about one we went out and made several calls. A most beautiful day. In the evening we went around to Mr. Maury's, spent a pleasant time.

<u>*Saturday, 28th.*</u> *It rained all day long. The Capt. and Mrs. Duval had a few warm words between them. I don't expect we will stay here much longer. I am trying to induce my Husband to try and get ordered to Texas.*

<u>*March 29th.*</u> *Palm Sunday. Father Huber preached a good sermon. After dinner I sat in the parlour. After Tea I called Mrs. Duval to my room and the Capt. and herself fixed the matter satisfactorily.*

April, 1863.

<u>Wednesday, the 1st. April.</u> I went to Church early. In the afternoon I went to Mr. Cook's to say Adieu to Mrs. Cranz who starts for Germany tomorrow.

Holy Thursday I went to Church at 8 O'clock and remained until 11 ½— they had a riot in the city this morn—men and women broke into stores and robbed.

After tea we went to Church again and heard a splendid sermon from the Bishop on the Eucharist, the Church was crowded.

Good Friday—I went to Church again. We had today the Adoration of the Cross. After Tea my Husband and myself went the stations of the Cross, after which we had a few feeling words from the Bishop.

Cousin Jeannie and Celeste came this evening.

Holy Saturday I went to Church at 8 O'clock, we had the blessing of the Holy Water.

<u>Sunday April 5th.</u> Easter. It is a very disagreable day, snowing and raining. I went out to Church at 8—went to Holy communion and returned at nine and half.

Monday, 13th. I have engaged a monthly nurse here for July. Miss Saunders, Mrs. Skinker and cousins spent the evening with us Monday.

Thursday, April 16th. Mrs. Pulaski spent the evening with us. Miss Morgan was to have come round but disappointed us. Cousin Jeannie and Celeste were dressed very prettily.

April 17th. Friday. We all went to the Theatre much to my dislike. The house is much prettier than I expected to find — the performance torably [sic] good. They played The Carpenter of Rouen.

We had a letter from Joe, they were all well at home, when he wrote March 11th —

Sunday, April 19th. A most lovely day. My Husband and myself got up early and went to Church at 8 O'clock. After that he went to Chapman's bluff with Major Williams for the day. In the evening we went around to Mrs. Nelson's.

Tuesday, 21st. We went around to Mrs. Maury's to spend the evening. Belle Maury made me some collars. I bought me a straw hat and trimmed it very prettily.

Wednesday, 22nd. A pleasant day. In the afternoon my Husband and myself walked to see Mrs. Col. Gorgas. We spent the evening with Mrs. James Purcell.

I received an English barege, shoes, corset and fine flannel from Maryland.

<u>*Sunday, 26th.*</u> *We went to Church at ten O'clock. Father Andrews preached a good sermon.*

<u>*Tuesday, 28th.*</u> *It rained nearly all day. My bonnet is finished, black lace, it cost $25. I furnished everything but the frame.*

<u>*Wednesday, 29th.*</u> *Gloomy in the morning. In the afternoon the Capt. got a buggy and we went out to Mrs. Pelaski's, It rained whilst we were on the road, but fortunately we did not get wet. I wrote home to Joe by Col. Wilcox.*

<u>*Thursday, 30th. April.*</u> *It poured down all night long, we remained at Mrs. P—'s. Capt. came into town about 10 O'clock and left me—*

May, 1863.

<u>Friday, 1st. May.</u> *A most lovely day. The enemy crossed, and were fighting near Fredericksburg yesterday. I came into town with Mrs. Pelaski. We had some delicious Ice cream and cake for dinner, it was the Anniversary of Mrs. Duval's wedding.*

After dinner I made several visits. The Capt. and Mrs. Garnet went out to the country to see a place where they offer us board—

<u>Saturday, 2nd.</u> *I went to Church early. I went out calling with Cousin Jeannie, came home quite tired.*

Gen. Lee's Army has defeated the Yankees again near Fredericksburg— May 4th. and 5th.

I again went to Church at 5 O'clock. After Tea the Capt. went round to the President's—

<u>Sunday, 3rd.</u> *We went to Church, after which I went home with Mrs. James Purcell. We came home at 4 O'clock, took a nap. In the evening we heard a hundred rumours about the Yankees coming to Richmond, only 15 miles from here, it is reported,—the people all seem to be **very much excited**. Cousin Jeannie speaks of going home day after tomorrow.*

Thursday, 7th. We made some calls. In the evening we went around to Mrs. Nelson's. I have been quite busy all the week preparing for summer.

Sunday, 10th. General Jackson died of his wounds and pneumonia. The great and noble hero will be a great loss to our country. Stonewall Jackson's remains will be brought down today, Monday.

Tuesday, 12th. Cousin Jeannie and Clement left here for Macon.

Gen. Jackson's remains were removed, they had an immense military procession through the streets, the stores and offices were all closed.

Wednesday I went to see Cousin Celeste, she was in bed—from there I went to Harriet Coleman's to have some sewing done.

Sunday, 17th. We went to Church at 8 O'clock. I have been to see Mrs. John Purcell who has a young baby.

It is reported that Jackson, Missis. has fallen.

Wednesday, 20th. My Husband got a buggy and took me to see Cousin Mary Grammer, Mrs. Stevens, and Gilmer,—in the afternoon after Tea we walked around to Dr. Harall's to sit with cousin John Grammer—

Capt. Semmes family of the Alabama are staying here. Mr. Buxton is very attentive to Miss Kate, sends her bouquets and all sorts of nice things every day.

Saturday, 23rd. *I did not walk out all day until evening. I dressed up and we went around to call on Mrs. Davis. Mrs. Tom Semmes came to see us.*

Sunday, 24th. *My Husband and myself got up early and went to early Church—he has gone out to Mrs. Grant's with other gentlemen to spend the day.*

It has been intensely warm all day. Mr. Buxton got some ice after dinner and gave us all some.

The Bishop has returned from the South. I am thinking of going up to Halifax on a visit in a few days.

May 28th. Thursday. *I started up to Halifax early in the morning with Uncle John Grammer and Cousin Mary Green, they were all very kind to me up there. I really enjoyed the change, the country was cool and delightful, plenty of ice and buttermilk. I wish I could have remained all the summer.*

I received letters from my Husband nearly every day. Cousin Celeste was extremely ill whilst I was gone.

June, 1863.

<u>Friday, 12th.</u> *I came to Richmond with Dr. T. Green. The Capt. met me at the Depot. I was really glad to get back, found Cousin Celeste much improved. Capt. Myers arrived here from Salisbury the same evening.*

<u>Saturday, 13th.</u> *A pleasant day. I walked around to see Cousin Celeste and Jeannie.*

<u>Sunday, 14th.</u> *The Capt. went to breakfast at Mr. Menard's and re-mained there until 1 O'clock. I went to Church at 10—Father Hagan preached. The Capt. went out again to dine at Judge Crump's, several gentlemen were invited— Mrs. Crump has had a mishap—In the evening Dr. Brewer walked around to see us and invited us to dine at his house the next day.*

<u>Monday, 15th.</u> *We have been married four years today. I walked up to Dr. Brewer's about 12 O'clock. Capt. Myers and my Husband dined with us, we had a delicious dinner and we enjoyed it.*

In the evening Capt. Myers took Cousin Jeannie and myself to Pezzinis—

I have had delightful news from home today, John Elliot has written to my Husband saying that Maria, my sister, was expected in San Antonio daily from Europe. It seems Father Dubuis has been made Bishop and brought her out.

Capt. Ingraham stayed in my room during my absence, he says Mrs. Whiting expects to be confined next month.

Tuesday, 16th. I did not go out in the morning. In the afternoon the Capt. took [me] to Mr. Menard's to see Lucy Gwinn. In the evening Capt. Myers and John Mitchell called. A friend sent us a little box full of splendid Strawberries which we enjoyed.

Wednesday, 17th. A warm day. I walked to see Mrs. Nelson and Cousin Celeste this morning. In the evening I went to see Mrs. Chilton and from [there] we walked to Major Williams and took Tea. On our return Capt. Myers took us to Antonis and treated us to ice cream.

Thursday, 18th. An intensely hot day. I did not venture out at all. Capt. Myers sent me an excellent Julep about 1 O'clock. In the evening we had a delightful rain. Alcée Toutant called to see me twice, but found me out both times. Gen. Lovell also called.

Wednesday, 24th. We walked around to see Cousin Jeannie who is going to leave for Macon this evening.

Poor Cousin Edmund lost his little twin daughter Bettie and Robert is also at the point of death.

Thursday, 25th. It rained all day long. I received some few things from Maryland today.

Friday, 26th. A gloomy day. General Lee's Army is in Maryland. In the morning I walked. In the afternoon I made one or two visits — spent the evening at Mrs. Grant's — The Yankees have made another cavalry raid.

Sunday, 28th. June. I went to Church at 8 O'clock — received Holy communion. After Church and breakfast the Captain went out to Camp to quiet some Mississippi troops that became insubordinate —

In the afternoon we walked around to John Purcell's and remained until after Tea. Monday it rained nearly all day.

July, 1863.

July 1st. Wednesday. We received a letter from Angel—they were all torably well at home when he wrote. I got up this morning feeling a little badly—walked out and remained all day at Mrs. James Purcell's, spent a pleasant day and had a good dinner. I came home and found a number of presents from friends—

Thursday, 2 July. There has been a deal of excitement in the city about Yankees coming. The Militia has been ordered out.

Mrs. John Purcell called on me. In the evening we walked out to Antonis and had some delicious ice cream. The weather is intensely hot—

July 3rd. A **very** hot day. The Militia is out again today. I felt very badly all the evening, retired about ten O'clock.

July 4th. 1863. Last night I did not rest well, I felt uncomfortable all night long,— waked up very early, sent for Dr. Dean before breakfast, he said there was no doubt but that I was in labour. Aunt Sally, the nurse, Mrs. Duval and my Husband were with me—the baby was born about a 15 minutes after eleven—not a Doctor was near me, Dr. Dean being engaged with Mr. Wall's wife who had a daughter on the same day.

Dr. Cunningham can to see me the first day—Dr. Talley was also sent for but was **too** late.

Our dear little Johnny is a fine little fellow, weighed nearly eight lbs. My friends were **exceedingly kind** to me, sending me **nice** things, and coming to see me. I had company nearly every day until I left Mrs. Duval's.

The Semmes left whilst we were there. The house was exceedingly **noisy** and disagreeable during my confinement, if it had not been for Mrs. Duval kindness we could have stood it.

Mrs. Tom Williams had a boy born on the same day as mine— likewise called after his Father.—

I heard my brother had a daughter born a month previous to mine.

We moved up to Mr. Starke's on the 1st. August, Saturday, we had an exceedingly hot spell when we first went up, however the change was pleasant, we live a good deal better. Mrs. Starke is very kind— the water we have up here is delightful.

August, 1863.

<u>August 15th. Saturday.</u> I had my baby christened today by the Bishop, who stood as god-father, and Miss Emily Mason God-Mother. We returned home and had some champagne and cake—

Mrs. Gen. Cooper came around.

Vicksburg fell on the day the baby was born—

September, 1863.

<u>September 1st.</u> We find it very pleasant at Mr. Starke's—

Tuesday we spent the day at Mrs. Tom Williams' very pleasantly. My boy is much larger than hers, fatter although born on the same day. Capt. Myers sent us a box of peaches.

The second Wed—We went to see Mrs. Duval and Mrs. Hall— Charlotte went back and Pattie came.

<u>Thursday, Sep. 3rd.</u> I find Pattie a most excellent servant and useful. We rode down to see Mrs. Nelson and Maury in the afternoon.

<u>Saturday, 5th.</u> I went to Confession and Communion on Sunday.

<u>Sep'r 8th. Tuesday.</u> We spent a very pleasant day at Mrs. John Purcell's—had a nice dinner and enjoyed everything—

<u>September 29th.</u> I had to send Pattie home, she was threatened with a miscarriage.

October, 1863.

<u>October 1st. Thursday</u>. We hired a girl that belonged to Col. Garnett to nurse Johnnie, Louisa is just from the country and seems to be a good servant—We have had a
great deal of trouble with servants, I have been worried to death—

<u>October 3rd. Saturday.</u> We moved to Mrs. Nelson's—we are elegantly fixed—better off than we ever have been in Richmond, in every respect. We occupy the whole of the third floor.

Mr. Menard was married on Monday 5th.—Capt. attended his wedding.

We have just received a box from sister with some wine and other little things—

Mr. Buxton, I understand, has been arrested.

<u>Saturday, 17th.</u> Mrs. Williams went up to Dr. Wayt's farm this morning.

We are very pleasantly fixed at Mrs. Nelson's. I went around to Mrs. Duval's and saw them all there. I took little Johnny there, nicely dressed, they all made a great fuss over him.

In the evening we went to Mr. Greenhow's.

There is a report that they are fighting up in the army.

Sunday, October 18th. I have just returned from Church. The Capt. I believe has gone to the country with Mr. Grant. A great many rumours on the street, the Militia is going up to Western Virginia.

I have not heard from my home for months.

October 23rd. Friday. Rather pleasant. I received three letters from home, one from Maria— all well. Joe has a boy named Edward, Concion one called Eugene. Grand doings at home—I wish I was at home. I feel very homesick.

Mrs. Williams child Tom was christianed today—she had several friends around there.

Mrs. Dangerfield finished my light poplin today—it wants altering very much. Dear little Johnny was sick yesterday, but better today— he has taken cold.

Sunday, November 1st. 1863. Feast of All Saints. A beautiful day. The Capt. is going out to the country to Mr. Grant's to spend the day.

We bought a servant yesterday, I trust she may suit us. Susan seems to be a good natured women, and says she is only eighteen—

I had several letters from home a few days ago, they were all well there.

Johnny is a fine healthy little boy — the poor little fellow will have to part with his nurse Louisa —

November— December, 1863.

<u>Nov. 28th.</u> Susan seems to get along pretty well. Johnny knows her already. I have had one of my dreadful sick headaches lately, I feel very weak from it.

I have Just been around to call on Mrs. Semmes who is our neighbor.

Mrs. and Captain Myers came from Salisbury to stay with us on 19th. December. We had a very pleasant time together, going every day.

On Christmas day Col. Williams and his family, Capt. Wade and Capt. Myers and wife dined with us. We had a mighty nice dinner—cake, Jelly, Blanc Mange and many nice things.

The gentlemen gave several parties. My Husband was invited to Mr. Grant's, Maury's and Dr. Cabell's.

Capt. and Mrs. Myers left us on the 4th. January, they hated to leave us and Richmond.

January, 1864.

January 4th. Johnny was six months old today.

January 5th. I am twenty five years old today. I had some cake and wine handed round.

Mr. Bunting from San Antonio called to see me. In the evening Myer Myers came to see us—

January 6th. Feast of the Epiphany. I went to Church at 10 O'clock—It is exceedingly cold today and snowing very fast. We are invited around to Mrs. Semmes this evening, they are going to have chirades [sic].

January 20th. We have had a most delightful spell of weather for two weeks past, mild and balmy and springlike, very unusual for this place at this season of the year—

Poor Mrs. Govan lost her only son, and Mrs. Branch her brother Mr. Bulkley. I attend the former funeral.

February, 1864.

<u>Feb. 1st. 1864.</u> The President and the Gov. both have been giving receptions for the last month—both places, I understand, have been well attended.

Mrs. Capt. Myers Sisters came a few days since. Maria and Martha are staying on Ross Street at the Myers'.

<u>Feb. 4th.</u> Johnny was seven months old today, he cannot sit alone yet—nor has he got a single tooth—the poor little fellow has taken a most wretched cold and cough and has been very restless at night.

Susan, I am afraid, is going to have a baby before very long—

The Capt. attended a play at Colonel Ives the other evening—Cousin Virginia and Celeste took part and acted their parts admirably well I am told. I could not go, not being very well, nor the baby well enough for me to leave him—

<u>Feb. 8th.</u> I attended a party at Mr. Sam Harrison's, it was very pleasant. We had an elegant supper. I was suffering with a bad cold then, and by the next day it was much worse—

Monday, Feb. 15th. Rather cold and damp we had a fall of snow. My cold is still quite bad. I have suffered a great deal with earache—a sort of neuralgia, I believe. Yesterday I was not well enough to go to Church even. Poor Colonel Wilcox died on Sunday last—Feb. 7th.—

Feb. 17th. Mr. Greenhow's little Samy died this morning. A bitter cold day it is. Last night the Capt. made me **some strange disclosures.**

February 25th. Thursday. A rather mild but a windy and disagreeable day—Dr. Dean came to see me this morning, he advises me to wean Johnnie and get a wet nurse if possible. I dislike it greatly, but I expect will have to do it.

Mrs. Myers sisters are coming around to spend this evening with us.

Johnny has cut his first two front tooth without any sickness, I am happy to say. We found them for the first time on Sunday last, the twenty first.

I would give a great deal to see my dear Mother, and relations once more, but I fear I will not be able until after the war.

March, 1864.

<u>Thursday, 3rd. March.</u> The Yankees made a grand raid near Richmond, expected to have captured and hung Jeff Davis and Cabinet, and set fire to Richmond. Their expedition failed altogether, thank God, and about three hundred of them were captured.

I went to see Mrs. George and John Maynard, Mrs. Major Norris, Mrs. Chilton.

<u>Friday, 4th.</u> My Johnny is eight months old today, he has been quite unwell for the last two days cutting teeth. I went to see Mrs. Finch, Mrs. Harrison, and Miss Webb.

I fear we will have to move again before long. Mrs. Nelson says she finds it very difficult to get provisions.

<u>Tuesday, March 8th.</u> The girl Mary came today, through all the rain, it made her quite sick for a day or two. Dr. Dean came to see her —

<u>March 9th.</u> We blind folded Johnny the first day and he nursed, but it frightened him —

<u>March 10th.</u> We can't coax Johnny to nurse — he won't do it.

Sunday, 13th. *Johnny nursed at last today. The Capt. went out to Mr. Grant to spend the day. Maria McRorie spent the day and went to Church with me. Miss Saunders married Capt. Contri.*

Tuesday, March 15th. *They are exchanging all of our prisoners —*

Poor Susan, Johnny's nurse left us today. I felt sorry for her.

Sunday, 19th. *Martha McRorie spent the day with me. In the afternoon I was taken sick with headache — the ladies went around to the square to see our returned prisoners. Johnny seem to enjoy it. I weaned my darling boy about the fifteenth and was taken sick at the same time.*

Monday, 21st. *Johnny was taken sick — I believe from his teeth.*

Tuesday, 22nd. *A dreadful day, snowing hard. Miss Page Waller was married to Major Page — I could not go to the Reception.*

Wednesday, Johnny continued sick, and would not stay with anybody but me.

Friday, 25th. Good Friday. *I went to Church. When I returned I heard Tommy Williams was extremely ill — Mrs. Ann Williams and myself went to see him and found him very low and suffering agony apparently. The little fellow died on Saturday and was buried on Easter Sunday, a beautiful day it was.*

My little darling has gotten quite well again.

Easter Sunday I went to Holy communion—In the evening Major Dashiel from Texas spent the evening with us.

Easter Monday, 28th. A pleasant day. We went out to Major Menard's and had an elegant lunch and delightful company—we did not return until nearly six.

April, 1864.

<u>April 1st.</u> We have had a great deal of rain all this month. The rivers rose very high.

We went over to Petersburg about the 18th. and remained there about ten days—I was sick nearly all the time, but notwithstanding all, I enjoyed my visit. Cousin Jeannie was **so** kind and sweet to me. We were invited out several times to spend the evening—and had splendid suppers. We had a **time getting back to R**.

Johnnie improved very much, gained several lbs. Major Dashiels left for Texas about three weeks ago. Poor Mrs. Brewer has lost her beautiful and only child. I feel deeply for her in her affliction.

<u>April 30th.</u> A **terrible** accident occurred yesterday—The President's little boy Joe was killed—fell from up stairs down in the erea [sic], a servant found the child first but already life had left him. His Mother and Father had walked out—

May, 1864.

<u>May 1st. 1864. Sunday.</u> We went to Church although it was raining. Father Huber preached about the blessed Virgin.

The President's child will be buried this evening.

<u>May 12th. Thursday.</u> I left Richmond for Mecklenburg with Mr. R. Russell. I did not intend going to the country until June, but the great excitement in Richmond, and my being sick, determined my Husband to send me sooner.

Mrs. Nelson left the day before for Dr. Wayt's, who was ill and gone deranged.

Gen. Lee's Army had been fighting Grant's for about a week before I left, and is still fighting I believe.

The Yankees attempted to advance on R—by different directions. Beauregard whipped them or checked them near Drewry Bluff—

Poor Gen. J. E. B. Stuart was wounded on the 11th. and died on the 12th May. I feel **so** much for his **poor wife**.

<u>May 21st.</u> I have been at Mrs. Russell's for about ten days. I like it very much, they are all very kind to me. It is a sweet place — beautiful scenery all around. I have not heard from the Capt. but once since I came.

Johnny is getting along finely, I put short clothes on him on the 10th. May — he did not take any cold from it.

June, 1864.

<u>June 20th</u>. *The Capt. came up to see us—having been sick he succeeded in getting a Furlough for six weeks.*

<u>Saturday, June 25th.</u> *The Capt. had not been with me many days when he and Mr. Russell had to go down to Roanoke bridge to defend it. The Yankees having made a raid advanced in large force to take it. The Capt. remained with the men during the fight, they repulsed the Yankees handsomely.*

The Enemy came within ten or eleven miles of Mr. Russell's place. A great many of the neighbours went on the other side of the river for safety. We were not much alarmed.

The gentlemen returned on Sunday 26th all safe and sound. I felt uneasy about them although I never dreamed that they had an engagement. We have had intensely hot weather.

July – August, 1864.

July 1st. A very warm day. We had a delightful little shower in the evening.

Johnny commenced to walk several days ago—and can say several words.

We have had a pleasant time at Mr. Russell's, all are very kind to us. We expect to go to Halifax on a little trip about Tuesday the 5th. I am anxious for our cousins to see Johnny.

July 4th. My boy is a year old today, he can walk a little, and has said a few words. We spent his birthday at Mr. Russell's.

Tuesday, 5th. We were invited to Dr. Venable's we spent quite a pleasant day.

July 6th. Wednesday. We went over to Halifax—found them all well and glad to see us, they were all mighty pleased with Johnny—he was not at all well when there, was threatened with croup, one night we were up with him nearly all night.

We remained in Halifax only about eight or nine days, as we had promised to visit Major and Mrs. Myers. On our way there we stopped to see Col. Withers family, they all treated me as a relative right away—

The Myers and McRories were glad to see us. We stayed with them a fortnight—returned to Mr. Russell about the 5th August. My Husband remained with me until the 12th, he then returned to Richmond to his business, suffering very much with boils.

Mrs. Ann Williams and Col. Williams came to Mr. R. about the 19th. of August, the Col. enjoyed the country exceedingly, but was obliged to return before his furlough expired on account of his wife, who was dissatisfied. I have enjoyed Mrs. Williams company very much.

September – November, 1864.

<u>Sept. 9 - 19th.</u> Mrs. Nelson came up on the 9th. Sept. I only heard of the death of my **sweet** sister about a week before Mrs. Nelson came up. It is a great comfort for me to know that my darling Maria died **so** happy and resigned to the Will of God, and cherishing such a sweet remembrance of her sister Anita.

My Husband knew of my sister's death two months before I heard of it— he feared I would grieve **too** much, and thereby injure my health.

The Capt. came up for us on the 17th, Saturday, and we returned on the 19th. Sept. from Mr. Russell's to Richmond. Mrs. Nelson and Williams remained at Mr. Crowders.

<u>Sept. 22nd.</u> I am now keeping house, Judy and myself make out pretty well at cooking—the Capt. seems well pleased. Some of my friends have already called on me. Mrs. Maury is going up to Dr. Wayt's tomorrow—

<u>Oct. 5th.</u> They [had] some fighting near Richmond about the 4th. and 5th. My Husband has gotten uneasy and determined to send me away again. Cousin John Brodnax has kindly invited me to his house in N. Carolina.

I concluded to send for Dr. Hughes, he prescribed for me. I was right in thinking I was more delicate than my friends imagined.

I started to Danville on the 12th. Oct.—exactly six months before I started for Meckenlenburg Co. I was very much opposed to leaving Richmond or rather my Husband, but he thought it the wisest course to pursue.

I remained in Danville only a week. Col. Withers family were all exceedingly kind to me—I was there when they moved to the bank—

I started for Cousin John's on the 20th. October—I have been here ten today—I am very much pleased, I like the household very much— Cousin Bettie is one of the sweetest women I ever saw. I have two servants here, Susan and Mary—

Mary was taken sick on Sunday 6th so I concluded it was a good time to wean Johnnie. I made Easter, one of the servants here, stay in my room at night. I had not had near as much trouble as I anticipated. Johnny cries for me nearly all the time.

<u>*Sunday, Nov. 13th*</u>*. I have been here nearly four weeks. I have enjoyed my stay here very well.*

I have taken Dr. Hughes medicine very regularly, I think it has done me some good.

Cousin John's Mother has been very ill since I came.

April, 1865.

<u>April 1st. 1865.</u> Saturday—A pleasant day. I exchanged nurses, I got Mary Heane from the sisters of Charity.

The 2nd. Sunday we went to Church, the Capt. went to Mr. Grant's farm afterwards. About two o'clock in the day Mr. Myers came around to Mrs. Nelson to inform the Capt. that Richmond was to be evacuated that afternoon.

Gen. Lee telegraphed Mr. Davis that the Yankees had broken through his lines in two different places and he feared would be compelled to give up Richmond and Petersburg.

My Husband did not return from the country until about 5 ½, he left me about seven and half.

The President, Cabinet and all the officers belonging to the different departments started on the Cars for Danville, Va. expecting to remain some there and defend that country. My Husband sometimes advised me to go to North Carolina or some other part of the Confederacy, but I refused, believing it best to remain in Richmond, thinking it would be the easiest way I could reach my home.

*I never spent **two such** nights in my life as I did the one of the evacuation and the one following, such fright, anxiety and dread I **never** before experienced. I felt sick for a week afterwards.*

April 3rd. The Yankees came into Richmond about nine O'clock in the morning. I moved up to Mr. Myer Myers the same day, they were all exceedingly kind to me, particularly Mr. Sol Myers. The Benjamins and The Crenshaws also invited me to stay with them. Mrs. Houseright stayed at the B. for some time.

My friends were all very kind in coming to see me. Mr. L. Crenshaw proved to be a good friend of ours.

Gen. Lee surrendered his army on the ninth of April, we southerners could scarcely believe it possible.

I heard from my dear Husband only once after we parted in Rich — he tells me to go home as soon as practicable. I started three weeks after the evacuation. Mr. G. T. Williams was my escort as far as New York, he was very attentive. We reached the city of N. York the very day that President Lincoln's remains passed through the city, the place seemed gayer and more crowded than ever. I saw Mr. and Mrs. Roumage several times.

I remained in New Orleans two weeks waiting to see if they would allow me to go by Galveston, — through the kindness of Gen'l Wilcox and Judge Hancock I succeeded in getting permission.

I remained in Houston about ten days waiting for my brother to come for me. I stayed at the McGreal's, they were very kind to me.

June — September, 1865.

<u>Sunday, June 4th</u>. I reached my dear home, my Mother of course was delighted to see me once more after a separation of nearly five years, she has given me a great many articles of clothing of hers and what belonged to my sweet sister.

<u>June 8th.</u> A great many old friends have come to see me. I find my Uncle Tom very much altered, looks about fifteen years older than when I last saw him. Joe and Annette are staying out at the Ranch with Mr. and Mrs. Joe Magoffin.

I have not heard one word from my dear Husband, I trust he may soon get here.

<u>Sunday, June 18th.</u> Joe, Annette and I went to the old church at ten o'clock. We had a good rain on our return home. Catarina and Carolina spent the day with us.

Poor Gen. Wilcox came to say farewell to me, he is about to start for Mexico with several other officers — they flee from their country on account of President Johnston proclamation —

My return to the Lone Star State dated June fourth 1865.

Poor Grandpapa died on the 6th. August.

My Husband returned August 14th. '65.

Josephine was born Sept. 7th. 1865.

Lt. Col. Withers' Military Career and Obituary

(From the *Twenty-Third Annual Reunion of the Association of the Graduates of the United States Military Academy*, pp. 76-81, June 9th, 1892.)

JOHN WITHERS.
No. 1429. CLASS OF 1849.
Died, February 3, 1892, in San Antonio, Texas, Aged 65.

There departed from this life on the 3d day of February, of this year, at San Antonio, Texas, a man as pure in life, as honest in purpose, as gentle and genial in disposition as ever falls to the character of poor mortals here below. His record on Cullum's Register of Officers and Graduates of the Military Academy reads as follows:

1429. (Born Ten.) JOHN WITHERS. (Ap'd. Mis.) 23.

Military History:-Cadet at the Military Academy July 1, 1844 to July 1, 1849, when he was graduated and promoted in the army to Brevet Second Lieutenant, Fifth Infantry, July 1, 1849.

Served: On frontier duty at Fort Gibson, Indian Territory, 1849-50; in garrison at (Second Lieutenant Fourth Infantry, January 31, 1850.) Detroit Barracks, Michigan 1850-51; Ft. Brady, Michigan, 1851-52, and Fort Columbus New York, 1852; on frontier duty at Benicia, California, 1852, Columbia Barracks, Washington, 1852-53 and at Ft. Vancouver, Washington, 1853-54; as Quartermaster Fourth Infantry, September 30, 1853 to September 10, 1856.

First Lieutenant Fourth Infantry, July 31, 1854.
Constructing Umpqua Valley Road, Oregon, 1854, and at Fort Vancouver, Oregon, 1854-55.

**Brevet Captain Staff-Assistant Adjutant General,
June 27, 1856.**
As Assistant Adjutant-General, Department of Texas, February 10, 1857 to June 10, 1859, and from December 21, 1859 to September 15, 1860; and as Assistant in the Adjutant General's Office at Washington, D. C., October 3, 1860 to March 1, 1861.

Resigned March 1, 1861.

Joined in the Rebellion of 1861-66 against the United States.

Civil History:--Cashier of the National Bank, of San Antonio, Texas, from 1871 to 1892.

In those days regiments had Colonels on paper, but rarely a Colonel with his regiment. Newman S. Clark, Colonel of the Sixth Infantry, was the only infantry Colonel who turned up in the Mexican War, and he was left to keep house at Vera

Cruz, but in the Fifth Infantry were such soldiers as Randolph B. Marcy, William Chapman and Frederick Dent, and the memories of Martin Scott and Ephriam Kirby Smith, lately killed at Molino del Rey were still fresh in the regiment, and the heroic deeds performed by the small, but powerful, regular army in the late Mexican war formed their topics of conversation at the mess table.

In 1852, Brevet Second-Lieutenant Withers became Second-Lieutenant Withers in the Fourth Infantry and served at Detroit, Michigan, and at Fort Brady, Michigan, until 1852, when the Fourth Infantry was concentrated at Fort Columbus, New York Harbor, and thence sailed by the Isthmus of Panama to California; Cholera broke out in the regiment and they were detained six weeks in camp on the Isthmus, and many men died; Captain John H. Gore was the only officer who succumbed to the dread disease. Lieutenant Withers was two years at Benicia Barracks; afterwards at Columbia Barracks and Vancouver. Lieutenant Withers was appointed Regimental Quartermaster of his regiment September 30, 1853; was First Lieutenant July, 54; was engaged in building the Umpqua Valley Road in 1854, and was appointed a Brevet-Captain in the staff and Assistant Adjutant-General, June 27, 1856.

The Fourth Regiment of Infantry, at the period that Withers joined it, and during the time he served with it, contained a remarkable list of officers; the regiment lost nine officers killed in the Mexican War, the greatest number lost in any regiment engaged in that war. Major George Wright was detailed to lead the forlorn hope of 500 men at the storming of

Molino del Rey. Amongst the survivors, who after related their trials and triumphs of the Mexican War to Lieutenant Withers, were Captain Robert C. Buchanan, Benjamin Alvord, Christopher C. Augur and Ulysses S Grant; and amongst the Lieutenants were Philip H. Sheridan, George Crook and Cadmus Wilcox. After Ulysses S. Grant became President of the United States, he found timber in the Fourth Infantry for four Brigadier-Generals in the United States Army.

Captain Withers was assistant Adjutant-General, Department of Texas, from February, '57 until September '60, when he was ordered to Washington for duty in the Adjutant-General's office, where he served until March 1, 1861, when he resigned his commission in the United States Army, and was appointed a Major in the Adjutant-General's Department of the Confederate Army. The following from the pen of Edward A. Palfrey, of New Orleans, a graduate of 1851, is in response to a letter of enquiry from me and is worthy of insertion:

> "Your letter of the 19th instant reached me this morning. Col. Jno. Withers was appointed Major and Assistant Adjutant General, June 5, 1861, at Montgomery; removed with the Confederate Government to Richmond, where he held the same rank until December 10, 1863, when he was appointed Lieutenant-Colonel, and held that rank until the fall of Richmond in 1865. His service was altogether in the Adjutant and Inspector General's Department at Richmond; he was in charge of the office next after General Cooper; his relations with the President and Sec-

retary of War were of an intimate character, as was necessarily the case from the position he held; his perfect familiarity with his duties, his untiring devotion to duty, and his great system, were of very great value, and it is certain that it would have been very hard to replace him; besides all this he was so uniformly courteous that such a thing as friction in the conduct of the business of his office was unknown.

At the fall of Richmond Colonel Withers left the city with the Government; upon arriving at Danville, the news of the surrender of his army reached him; the Adjutant and Inspector General's offices were closed and Colonel Withers started for the Trans-Mississippi, was captured by Cavalry, Palmer's (W. J.) Division, at Athens, Georgia, was paroled, and proceeded thence to San Antonio.

I trust that this memorandum will serve you; his salient characteristics were a cool and determined courage, a quiet, painstaking devotion to such duties as were set before him, and a perfect integrity.

I am much pleased to hear from you, and hope that your memories of the association of our youth may be as pleasant as mine are. I am

Your old comrade,
ED. A. PALFREY."

Colonel Withers married in San Antonio in June, 1857 [1859]; his wife was Miss Anita Dwyer, the daughter of a very distinguished citizen of San Antonio, and who was connected with the exciting scenes that delivered Texas from Mexican rule and Indian terror. The cause of the Confederacy being lost, Colonel Withers returned to the home of his wife; he engaged in mercantile business with the late Thomas G. Williams, a classmate and a graduate of West Point, as a partner; their business was a success, but getting a call to the position of Cashier of the San Antonio National Bank, Colonel Withers accepted the position and most faithfully filled it up to the day of his death. This bank has been a very successful institution, and as the President of the bank spent much of his time away, the management fell largely on Colonel Withers. His integrity and his perfect amiability and good manners brought custom. The Colonel possessed a competency, but not riches, as matters go now-a-days, but he was always foremost in public enterprises and benevolent movements; he was an active promoter of the Aransas Pass Railroad, was Treasurer of the San Antonio Club, President of St. Vincent de Paul Society, and was the trusted friend of the widow and the many who did not know what to do with their money; they always wanted John Withers to keep it for them.

Withers was an all-around man; his leading characteristic was cheerfulness; he was always ready with a good-natured joke, but, business requiring, he could stop the laugh and strike the key to business as quickly as any solemn money dealer; he was strictly pious and a constant attendant at church. We who knew him best, miss him as no words of mine can tell.

He left a wife and six children, four sons and two daughters; the eldest daughter is the wife of Captain John L. Bullis, Twenty-Fourth Infantry, well known for his services on the Indian frontier; the youngest daughter is not yet grown; the boys are all single and engaged in business.

Soldier, merchant, banker, companion, friend and Christian, he was worthy of his Alma Mater, and added in his life another unit to the great mass of solid characters which make the glory of our Academy.

D. S. STANLEY.

Significant Names

Adjutant General in Washington D.C. until March 7, 1861; Samuel Cooper.

Anderson; Major Robert Anderson—In command of Fort Sumter at start of Civil War (April 1861); promoted to Brigadier General of Union Army on May 15, 1861.

Beall; William (Billy) N.R. Beall—Brigadier General for the Confederacy; captured with surrender of Port Hudson in 1862, paroled, but never exchanged; in 1864 became known for his efforts to provide supplies for Confederate prisoners of war in northern prison camps.

Buchanan; President James Buchanan—15th President of the United States; 1857 – 1861.

Brown's Hotel—aka Brown's Marble Hotel (1851); later known as the Metropolitan Hotel; located on Pennsylvania Avenue in Washington, D.C.

Cass; General Lewis Cass—22nd U.S. Secretary of State; resigned December 14, 1860.

Clay; (Cousin)   Clement Claiborne Clay (and Virginia Clay (aka Cousin Jeannie)); U.S. Senator for state of Alabama; later Confederate States Senator for Alabama; charged with complicity in the murder of President Lincoln; held at Fortress Monroe for one year, and then released, due to the efforts of his wife.

Cooper; Colonel (later General) Samuel Cooper— Adjutant General of the U.S. Army (resigned March 7, 1861; six days after dismissing Brig. Gen. David E. Twiggs from the Army); highest ranking Confederate General during Civil War.

Davis; Jefferson Davis—U.S. Secretary of War under President Franklin Pierce; U.S. Senator for the state of Mississippi; President of the Confederated States of America.

Dwyer; Major Joseph (Joe) E. Dwyer—(March 1, 1841-Sept. 14, 1884); served one term in the Texas state senate; represented Texas in four National Democratic conventions; chairman of the congressional executive committee and chairman of the county executive committee.

Fitzpatrick; Governor Fitzpatrick (Benjamin Fitzpatrick)— Governor of Alabama; United States Senator for the state of Alabama.

Floyd; Secretary John B. Floyd—24th United States Secretary of War; March 6, 1857 – December 29, 1860.

Julius Peter Garesché—Captain in the War Department; wanted to serve on field of battle for the Union, and requested transfer for field duty several times; eventually succeeded in transferring to position of General Rosecran's Chief of Staff in November 1862; gallant on the field of battle; while riding out reforming lines with General Rosecrans, was decapitated by a cannonball and killed on December 31, 1862.

Harney; General (William S.) Harney—U.S. Army cavalry officer.

Hill; Lt. A.P. (Ambrose Powell) Hill—U.S. army; later became a successful Lieutenant General in the Confederate Army. Served under Stonewall Jackson and Robert E. Lee.

Johnston; General A.S. (Albert Sidney) Johnston—Texas army General, and Confederate States General; killed in the Battle of Shiloh, 1862.

Johnston; General Joe E. Johnston—U.S. Army officer; later became one of the senior Generals for the Confederacy during the Civil War; on April 26, 1865, he surrendered his armies to Sherman.

Magruder; Capt. W. T. Magruder—Fought as a Union Captain for the 1st U.S. Cavalry until October 1, 1862; joined Confederate Army as a Captain; died at Gettysburg.

Palfrey; Major (later) Lt. Col. Edward A. Palfrey; Assistant Adjutant General in the Adjutant General's Department, War Office of the Confederacy in Richmond, VA.

Prince of Wales, Baron Renfrew (Edward Albert VII); 19 years old when visited United States and Canada in fall of 1860.

Randolph: George W. Randolph; Secretary of War for the Confederacy; Thomas Jefferson's grandson.

Scott; General Winfield Scott— Commanding General of the United States Army for twenty years; he was an active duty General for 47 years.

Spotswood Hotel—Richmond, VA; was located at southeast corner of 8th and Main streets; burned down in a fire in 12/26/1870.

Stevens; Governor Stevens (Isaac Ingalls Stevens)—first Governor of Washington Territory; later became Brigadier General for the Union Army, and died in the Battle of Chantilly on September 1, 1862.

Thompson; Jacob Thompson— United States Secretary of the Interior, 1857 – 1861.

Toombs, Brigadier General Robert Augustus Toombs—U.S. Senator for the state of Georgia; the first Secretary of State for the Confederacy; Brigadier General in the Confederate Army.

Wayne; Judge Wayne (James Moore Wayne)—served on the U.S. Supreme Court from 1835 to 1867.

Willard's Hall (Willard Hotel)—1401 Pennsylvania Avenue NW, Washington, D.C.; Abraham Lincoln stayed there from February 23 – March 4, 1861. (Just before and up until his presidential inauguration.)

Winder; Brigadier General John Henry Winder—was commissary-general for the Confederacy for prisoners east of the Mississippi River. He died February 7, 1865.

Medical Terms

Blue mass—Used as a common remedy for many illnesses, including tuberculosis, toothache, etc. The ingredients varied by the pharmacist that made it, but all included some form of mercury (elemental) or mercury compound (mercury chloride, also known as *calomel*).

Dover's powder—"DOVER'S POWDER is a preparation of powder of ipecacuanha 1 drachm, opium in powder 1 drachm, and sulphate of potash 1 ounce. The whole is thoroughly mixed, and the ordinary dose is from 6 to 10 grains. Occasionally, saltpetre is added." (Chambers)

Erysipelas—A skin infection (cellulitis), often caused by group A *Streptococcus* bacteria.

Intipsicated—Intoxicated/Drunk.

Paregoric—Camphorated tincture of opium. Used as an antidiarrheal, cough suppressant and analgesic.

Tartar Emetic—consists of antimony and potassium tartrate. Was used as an emetic (to induce vomiting) and expectorant, and to produce sweating. Frequent toxic side effects.

Lt. Col. John Withers' Genealogy

(Names in bold are mentioned in the diary entries.)

i.> John Withers (1772-1826), who resided in Dinwiddie County in 1800, married Mary Herbert Jones (Mar. 12, 1777-1848), and they moved to Madison County, Alabama. They had the following children:

– *John Wright Withers (Dr.)*, (1796- 15 Mar. 1836) married Palmyra Scott Jordan.

– *Susanna Claiborne Withers* (23 July 1798 - 1866) married Clement Comer Clay, Chief Justice of Alabama at age thirty, Governor of Alabama, Congressman, U. S. Senator. One of their sons was

Clement Claiborne Clay (December 13, 1817-January 3, 1881). He was a U.S. Senator, Senator of Confederate States, Member of Confederate Cabinet, and Commissioner of Confederate States to Canada. At the close of the Civil War, he and Jefferson Davis, President of the Southern Confederacy, were by the United States arrested as rebels and as the two foremost leaders of the rebellion, and were imprisoned for a number of months at Fortress Monroe, in Virginia. He was subsequently released without trial. He married **Virginia Tunstall** (later known as Virginia Clay-Clopton), a beauty and wit, on February 1, 1843,

Tuscaloosa,Tuscaloosa County, Alabama. They had no children. *(These two are Cousin Clement and Cousin Jeannie)*

ii.> – *William Frederick Withers*, (February 29th, 1800-1849/50); married (a) in 1826 Catherine Hawkins, born September 22nd, 1804, by whom he had six children; and (b) Harriet Carter in 1846, by whom he had two children. He died in 1849 or 1850 in Texas.

– *David Wright Withers* served in the Eighty-third Regiment during the War of 1812.

– *Priscilla Wright Withers*

– *Augustine Jones Withers*

– *Ann Eliza Ward Withers* married **Francis John Levert** 14 November 1838 in Madison County, Alabama.

– *Mary Dorothy Mitchell Withers*

– *Jones Mitchell Withers* (12 Jan. 1814 - 13 Mar. 1890). Major General for Confederacy, politician and Mayor for Mobile, Alabama.

– *Maria Herbert Withers* (1818- 22 Nov. 1867) married Rev. Anastasius Menaeos.

ii.> *William Frederick Withers* (Feb. 29, 1800-1849/50) married Catherine Hawkins (first wife), in 1826 in Bexar Co, Texas. (In 1846 he married Harriet Carter.) Catherine and William had the following children:

iii.> – *Col. John Withers* (Feb. 22, 1827-Feb. 3, 1892)

– *Susanna Claiborne Clay*, born July 13th, 1829.

– **William Frederick**, July 29, 1832.

– *Caleb Hawkins*, August 30, 1835.

– *Mary McClelland*, May 4, 1837.

– *Catherine Hawkins*, June 24, 1839.

– *Clement Augustine*, February 5, 1842.

iii.> Col. John Withers, (Feb. 22, 1827-Feb. 3, 1892), born in Lexington, TN, married ***Anita Dwyer*** (January 5, 1839-June 5, 1909), daughter of Edward and Mariana Dwyer, in Bexar County, Texas on June 15, 1859. They had the following children:

– ***Edward Dwyer Withers***, (March 22, 1860-July 20, 1861)
– *John Withers*, (July 4, 1863-1892)
– *Josephine* Withers *Bullis*, (September 7, 1865-1934)
– *William Frederick Withers*, (1867-1895)
– *Robert Lee Withers*, (1869-1927)
– *Clement Clay Withers*, (1872-1892)
– *Anita* Withers *Russell*, (1875-1913)

Anita Dwyer Withers' Genealogy

i.> Edward Dwyer (Nov. 5, 1808-April 27, 1857), from County Dublin, Ireland, married Mariana Leal Dwyer (1809-July 17, 1867), from San Antonio, Texas. They had the following children:

ii.>– Anita Leal Dwyer Withers, (January 5, 1839-June 5, 1909) married John Withers. (Listed previously--please see John Withers' entry for the names of their children.)
– Major Joseph Edward Dwyer, (March 1, 1841-Sept. 14, 1884); married Annette Magoffin.
– Thomas Anthony Dwyer, (1843-1853)
– Edward Dwyer, (1846-1846)
– Maria Dwyer, (1847-1863)

Examples of Orders Written by Lt. Col. John Withers

(Source: United States War Department. *THE WAR OF THE REBELLION: A Compilation of the Official Records of the Union and Confederate Armies*. Washington: Government Printing Office, 1880-1901.)

p. 44-45
SPECIAL ORDERS,
ADJT. AND INSP. GENERAL'S OFFICE, Numbers 45.
Richmond, February 25, 1862.
* * * *

XVIII. Major-General Magruder will so dispose of the forces under his command and make necessary preparations as to be able to move across the James River all forces that can be spared from his batteries and intrenchments to co-operate in the repulse of the enemy from any threatened attack on Suffolk or other approaches to Norfolk. He will have is forces in readiness to cross the river on receiving further orders.
* * * *

By command of the Secretary of War:
JNO WITHERS,
Assistant Adjutant-General.

p. 597
ADJUTANT AND INSPECTOR-GENERAL'S OFFICE,
Richmond, Va., June 13, 1862.

It is necessary for the War Department to impress slaves to complete certain fortifications for the protection of the country. The citizens of Halifax, Lunenburg, Charlotte, Pittsylvania, and Campbell Counties are therefore called upon the send forthwith one-fourth of their male slaves between the ages of sixteen and fifty to execute this work in the vicinity of Richmond. The negroes will be paid for at the rate of $10 per month each, and receive an ample supply of provisions [rate of compensation changed to $20 per month by order of the Secretary of War], the money to be paid by the Engineer Department to their masters promptly at the places where they may work. The cost of transportation to be paid by the Government.

The bearer of his, Captain William Turnbull, is authorized to give receipts for the negroes, and from the dates of said receipts the Government of the Confederate States will be responsible for the slaves according to the laws of Virginia, with the additional responsibility for their value, should they escape to, or be injured by, the enemy. These negroes will be sent to the nearest railroad depots, in accordance with instructions to be given by the agent. Cost of transportation will be paid upon the production of evidence, signed by the agent, that it has been furnished. In order to facilitate the collection of the negroes the Government agent may appoint sub-agents from among the owners of slaves in the counties called upon, two of whose negroes will be released as compensation for their labor.

By command of the Secretary of War:
JNO WITHERS,
Assistant Adjutant-General.

p. 653
SPECIAL ORDERS,
ADJT. AND INSP. GENERAL'S OFFICE, Numbers 139. Richmond, June 15, 1864.
* * * *

XII. Major James M. Quinlan, commissary of subsistence, on duty as post commissary at Columbus, Miss., will turn over all stores and property in his possession to Major R. H. Cuney, commissary of subsistence, chief purchasing commissary at Columbus, Miss., and will report by letter of Major W. H. Dameron, chief commissary of subsistence for Mississippi, for assignment to duty at Okolona, Miss., to relieve Captain B. J. Martin, assistant commissary of subsistence. Captain Martin, on being relieved, will report to Major Dameron, at Meridian, for assignment to duty.
* * * *

By command of the Secretary of War:
JNO WITHERS,
Assistant Adjutant-General.

p. 774
SPECIAL ORDERS,
ADJT. AND INSP. GENERAL'S OFFICE, Numbers 15.
Richmond, January 18, 1862.
* * * *

XIV. The 250 C. S. troops (10 officers, 240 privates and non-commissioned officers) who were captured by the U. S. troops at Hatteras, N. C., subsequently released from Fort Warren, Boston Harbor, and released on parole by General Wool, U. S. Army, are hereby released from said parole an will immediately report for duty with their respective companies, General Wool having acknowledged in exchange the receipt of a like number of U. S. prisoners sent to Fortress Monroe, Va., by the Confederate States Government.

By command of the Secretary of War:
JNO WITHERS,
Assistant Adjutant-General.

p. 1117
SPECIAL ORDERS,
ADJT. AND INSP. GENERAL'S OFFICE, NO. 268.
Richmond, November 10, 1864.
* * * * * *

XIV. The prisoners recently brought in by the Tallahassee at Wilmington, N. C., will be sent to Florence, to be there held until exchange or discharged.
* * * * *

By command of the Secretary of War:
JNO WITHERS,
 Assistant Adjutant-General.

Statement of Copyright

Bibliography

"Abraham Lincoln at the Willard Hotel." *Abraham Lincoln Online: Historic Places*. 2010. Web. 25 Feb. 2011. <http://showcase.netins.net/web/creative/lincoln/sites/willards.htm>.

"ADJUTANT AND INSPECTOR-GENERAL." *AFRICAN AMERICAN MILITARY HISTORY*. United States War Department. THE WAR OF THE REBELLION: A Compilation of the Official Records of the Union and Confederate Armies. Washington: Government Printing Office, 1880-1901. Web. 03 Mar. 2011. <http://www.lwfaam.net/cw/csaltr/withers1.htm>.

Bigg-Wither, Reginald Fitz Hugh. *Materials for a History of the Wither Family*. Winchester [Eng.: Warren & Son, 1907. 171-172. Print.

Boddie, John Bennett. "Claiborne of England and Virginia." *Virginia Historical Genealogies*. Baltimore, MD: Reprinted for Clearfield by Genealogical, 2008. 42. Print.

"Brigadier–General John H. Winder, C. S. A." *The Photographic History of the Civil War: Volume 7 - Prisons and Hospitals.* 24 May 2006. Web. 27 Feb. 2011. <http://www.pddoc.com/photohistory/v7/102.htm>.

Cassidy-Dwyer, Melissa. "Joseph Edward Dwyer (1841 - 1884)." *Find A Grave - Millions of Cemetery Records.* 15 June 2010. Web. 02 Mar. 2011. <http://www.findagrave.com/cgi-bin/fg.cgi?page=gr&GRid=53720346>.

Chambers's Encyclopædia: a Dictionary of Universal Knowledge for the People. Vol. III. London: W. & R. Chambers, 1886. Page. 651. Print.

"The Claiborne Family." *Our Southern Cousins.* 3 Mar. 2007. Web. 26 Feb. 2011. <http://oursoutherncousins.com/CLAIBORNE%20FAMILY.pdf>.

Clay-Clopton, Virginia. *A Bell of the Fifties: Memoirs of Mrs. Clay, of Alabama, Covering Social and Political Life in Washington and the South, 1853-1866.* New York: Doubleday, Page & Company, 1905, c1904. *Documenting the American South.* 1998. Academic Affairs Library, The University of North Carolina at Chapel Hill. 24 February 2011. 188-189. <http://docsouth.unc.edu/fpn/clay/clay.html>.

Cowan's Auctions. "A Large Collection of North Carolina Confederate Supply Returns and Other Official Papers, - Cowan's Auctions." *Cowan's Auctions*. 2008. Web. 26 Feb. 2011.
<http://www.cowanauctions.com/auctions/item.aspx?item id=60116>.

Davenport, Jim. "Col John Withers (1827 - 1892)." *Find A Grave - Millions of Cemetery Records*. 12 Feb. 2010. Web. 26 Feb. 2011.
<http://www.findagrave.com/cgi-bin/fg.cgi?page=gr&GRid=48041097>.

"Descendants of John Comer." *Family Tree Maker's Genealogy Site*. 2009. Web. 28 Feb. 2011.
<http://familytreemaker.genealogy.com/users/w/h/i/Robert-C-Whitehead-GA/GENE2-0011.html>.

"eHistory at OSU | Search." *EHistory at OSU | Welcome to EHistory*. THE WAR OF THE REBELLION: A Compilation of the Official Records of the Union and Confederate Armies. United States War Department. Washington: Government Printing Office, 1880-1901. Web. 02 Mar. 2011.
<http://ehistory.osu.edu/osu/search/searchAction_OR.cfm?keyWords=jno. withers>.

"Erysipelas - Symptoms, Diagnosis, Treatment of Erysipelas - NY Times Health Information." *Health News - The New York Times*. A.D.A.M., Inc. Web. 02 Mar. 2011. <http://health.nytimes.com/health/guides/disease/erysipel as/overview.html>.

Garesché, Louis. *Biography of Lieut. Col. Julius P. Garesché, Assistant Adjutant-General, U.S. Army*. Philadelphia: J.B. Lippincott, 1887. Print.

Gibson, Steve. "The Granado Family from Lanzarote Island, the 14th Family of the List of Canary Islanders Taken at Quautitlan, November 8, 1730, Descendants of Juan Rodriguez Granado. [283. Anita Dwyer]." *Bexar Genealogy*. 21 Aug. 2010. Web. 28 Feb. 2011. <http://webcache.googleusercontent.com/search?q=cache: o- MaG340IIQJ:bexargenealogy.com/archives/familyfiles/gra nado.rtf+%22clement+clay+withers%22+%2B+1892&cd=12 &hl=en&ct=clnk&gl=us&source=www.google.com>.

McCabe, W. Gordon. "Southern Historical Society Papers: Graduates of West Point Serving in the CSA Army." *The Civil War Home Page*. Web. 25 Feb. 2011. <http://www.civil-war.net/searchshsp2.asp?search=Graduates of West Point Serving in the CSA Army>.

"The Metropolitan, Aka Brown's Marble Hotel." *Streets of Washington*. 10 Dec. 2009. Web. 25 Feb. 2011. <http://streetsofwashington.blogspot.com/2009/12/metropolitan-aka-browns-marble-hotel.html>.

Owen, Thomas McAdory, and Marie Bankhead Owen. "Dictionary of Alabama Biography." *History of Alabama and Dictionary of Alabama Biography*. Vol. 3. Chicago: S.J. Clark, 1921. 341-42. Print.

Read, Allen W. "Intipsicated" *Pseudodictionary: the Dictionary for Words That Wouldn't Make It into a Real Dictionary :: V2.0*. Web. 02 Mar. 2011. <http://www.pseudodictionary.com/search.php?letter=i&browsestart=520>.

"Records of Lt. Col. John Withers." *The National Archives*. Web. 17 Feb. 2011. <http://research.archives.gov/arcdataviewer/faces/showDetail?file=Series_2524414.xml&loc=456>.

"Spotswood Hotel." *Civil War Richmond*. 17 July 2008. Web. 25 Feb. 2011. <http://www.mdgorman.com/Other_Sites/spotswood_hotel.htm>.

Stanley, D. S. "John Withers - Obituary Notice (Association of Graduates USMA, 1892)." *Sir Thomas Browne*. Bill Thayer, 27 Nov. 2010. Web. 23 Feb. 2011. <http://penelope.uchicago.edu/Thayer/E/Gazetteer/Places/America/United_States/Army/USMA/AOG_Reunions/23/John_Withers*.html>.

Stanley, D. S. "Twenty-Third Annual Reunion of the Association of the Graduates of the United States Military Academy, at West Point, New York, June 9, 1892." *USMA Library's Digital Collections*. United States Military Academy Library at West Point. Web. 2 Mar. 2011. Pages 76-81.<http://digital-library.usma.edu/libmedia/archives/aogreunion/V1892.PDF>.

"Tartar Emetic." <u>The Columbia Encyclopedia, Sixth Edition</u>. 2008. *Encyclopedia.com*. 17 Mar. 2011 <http://www.encyclopedia.com>.

"Tartar Emetic." *Encyclopædia Britannica. Encyclopædia Britannica Online*. Encyclopædia Britannica, 2011. Web. 17 Mar. 2011. <http://www.britannica.com/EBchecked/topic/583758/tartar-emetic>.

Tolliver, Donna L. "Edward Dwyer (1808 - 1857)." *Find A Grave - Millions of Cemetery Records*. Web. 28 Feb. 2011. <http://www.findagrave.com/cgi-bin/fg.cgi?page=gr&GRid=17996805>.

Tolliver, Donna L. "Mariana Leal Dwyer (1809 - 1867)." *Find A Grave - Millions of Cemetery Records.* 29 Oct. 2008. Web. 03 Mar. 2011. <http://www.findagrave.com/cgi-bin/fg.cgi?page=gr&GRid=30959668>.

Various. *Wikipedia, the Free Encyclopedia.* Web. 25 Feb. 2011. <http://en.wikipedia.org/wiki/>.

VKN. "Clement Claiborne Clay~of Interest." *Reconstruction Period Research Forum.* 14 May 2004. Web. 26 Feb. 2011. <http://www.afrigeneas.com/forum-reconstruction/index.cgi/md/read/id/137/sbj/clement-claiborne-clay-of-interest/>.

Webmaster Ann. "Brigadier General William N. R. Beall." *American Civil War.* 20 Sept. 2007. Web. 27 Feb. 2011. <http://www.factasy.com/civil_war/content/brigadier-general-william-n.-r.-beall>.

Withers, Anita Dwyer. Diary of Anita Dwyer Withers, Diary, 1860-1865. Transcript of manuscript #1746-Z, Southern Historical Collection, Academic Affairs Library, University of North Carolina at Chapel Hill. *Documenting the American South.* 1999. Academic Affairs Library, The University of North Carolina at Chapel Hill. 18 February 2011. <http://docsouth.unc.edu/imls/withers/withers.html>.

Zemanta. "The Gallant Garesché." *Civil War Murfreesboro: A Guide to Murfreesboro, Tennessee During the War.* 5 May 2010. Web. 25 Feb. 2011. <http://www.civilwarmurfreesboro.com/2010/05/05/the-gallant-garesche/>.

www.ingramcontent.com/pod-product-compliance
Lightning Source LLC
Chambersburg PA
CBHW021901020426
42334CB00013B/426